MEDITATION
What It Can Do for You

MEDITATION
What It Can Do for You

Daniel Cohen
Illustrated with photographs and reproductions

DODD, MEAD & COMPANY
New York

ILLUSTRATION CREDITS

The illustrations in this book are used by permission and through the courtesy of the following: New York Public Library Picture Collection, x, 2, 10, 19, 25, 27, 30, 32, 89, 103, 108, 110; Religious News Service Photos, 13, 28, 43 120; United Press International Photos, 21, 76, 82; Wide World Photo, 121.

The Sufi tales are from books by Idries Shah: Page 31, from *Thinkers of the East*, published by Penguin Books, 1972. Reprinted by permission of Curtis Brown, Ltd., copyright © 1971 by Idries Shah. Pages 109–111, from *Wisdom of the Idiots*, published by E. P. Dutton, 1971. Reprinted by permission of Curtis Brown, Ltd., copyright © 1969 by Idries Shah. Page 104, from *The Book of the Book*, published by Octagon Press, London, 1969. Reprinted by permission of A. P. Watt & Son, copyright © 1969 by Idries Shah.

Copyright © 1977 by Daniel Cohen
All rights reserved
No part of this book may be reproduced in any form without permission in writing from the publisher
Printed in the United States of America

1 2 3 4 5 6 7 8 9 10

Library of Congress Cataloging in Publication Data

Cohen, Daniel.
    Meditation.
    SUMMARY: Defines and surveys its history and various forms, and focuses on Transcendental Meditation.
    Bibliography: p.
    Includes index.
    1. Meditation—Juvenile literature.
2. Transcendental meditation—Juvenile literature.
[1. Meditation. 2. Transcendental meditation]
I. Title.
BF637.M4C63   158   77-7499
ISBN 0-396-07471-5

To Arvis and Angela Stewart

Contents

1	What Is Meditation?	1
2	The Range of Meditation	8
3	TM—The Big One	38
4	TM vs. RR	59
5	Meditation and the Brain	73
6	Fears and Fantasies	86
7	Meditation and Miracles	105
8	Meditation, Mysticism, and the Right Hemisphere	116
9	Life Is a Fountain	130
	Bibliography	135
	Index	139

Most forms of meditation involve sitting quietly.

1

What Is Meditation?

If you are not "doing" meditation yourself, you very well may know someone who is. About six million Americans are engaged in the most popular form of meditation, according to a 1976 Gallup survey. Millions more are involved in other meditative practices.

Meditation—ten years ago, one practically never heard the word in America. Today practically everyone has heard of it. When you say the word most people will immediately think of a person sitting quietly, eyes closed, and silently repeating over and over a *mantra* or secret word. Most people would also say that meditation is a practice brought to the West from India.

That description fits one form of meditation, admittedly the most well-publicized and popular form in the United States at this moment. But it is only part of the meditation picture.

Most meditation does involve sitting quietly. But the meditator may sit in a chair, or cross-legged upon the floor or be in a kneeling position. Some silently repeat a mantra, while

MEDITATION: WHAT IT CAN DO FOR YOU

others may count their breaths or focus their mind on attempting to answer a question that has no rational answer. For example, "What is the sound of one hand clapping?"

Some meditators prefer to keep their eyes open, and focus their attention on an object. It may be a religious object like a cross or icon, a secular object like a vase or rock, or simply a blank wall or a point in space. Some may imagine a white light or picture a bubble rising in a tank of water.

Meditation is not necessarily either still or quiet. It can involve repeating a phrase quietly but audibly and rocking back and forth, or fingering a string of beads. Other forms of meditation may require loud chanting or singing, whirling about,

Some forms of meditation may require loud chanting or singing, whirling about, or wild dancing.

2

WHAT IS MEDITATION?

or wild dancing, until the individual literally drops from exhaustion.

Finally, there are forms of meditation which most of us would find repellent, or "sick." These may take the form of long peroids of fasting, subjecting the body to harsh and uncomfortable conditions, or deliberately inducing pain by whipping, sticking needles in the flesh, and other types of self-torture. One definition of meditation is concentration with a spiritual objective. But one can concentrate on anything, even pain.

The result of these various techniques, from the mild to the terrifying, is a dramatic change in the focus of attention. The ordinary way in which the mind of an individual relates to the outside world and to his own thoughts and emotions is changed. Today consciousness is a popular word and we often hear that meditation induces an "altered state of consciousness."

None of these techniques are random or unplanned. Meditation may be natural to human beings, as some claim, but it doesn't "just happen." It always involves a degree of discipline and training, often a very high degree of both.

While the current popularity of meditation in the West is due primarily to techniques imported from India, and to a lesser extent from Japan, meditation is not exclusively Indian or Japanese, or even Eastern. Both Christianity and Judaism have developed their own traditions of meditation.

Most meditative practices are very ancient, but some startling new ones have been developed within this century. Generally, meditation is part of a religious practice, but not necessarily. Many nonreligious people meditate, and quite recently scientists have become interested in the practice and have, through experiment, been able to revise ancient practices in line with what they consider scientifically sound principles.

MEDITATION: WHAT IT CAN DO FOR YOU

What is it all for, this experience which has commanded the attention of so much of humanity for so long? For many Americans meditation is primarily a technique for reducing stress and tension. A variety of tests have indicated that meditation can produce a restful state that can have beneficial physiological effects. That is how most scientists became interested in the subject. The techniques that they have developed are aimed solely at producing this relaxed state. Some traditional meditative practices sound, at first, as if that is what they are aiming at as well. But most meditation is aimed at something more than relaxation.

Meditators often say that the discipline and the tranquillity of mind it produces helps them to organize their lives better, and that through meditation they have become more fulfilled, creative, and generally happier. But even that is just the beginning.

Beyond improvements in health and daily life, there is a vast area that we might loosely call mysticism that is approached through meditation. The aim of most meditative practices throughout history has been to help the individual reach a state that is beyond the ordinary day-to-day life.

When discussing these higher or perfected states of meditation one plunges into a jungle of terminology which is vague, confusing, and often contradictory. Some meditators would object to the term "higher or perfected state of meditation" or even to the use of the word "meditation."

Meditators often speak of "greater self-awareness" that comes through the practice. Some speak of "enlightenment," but this may also be described as a state in which the mind is perfectly blank. Modern meditators use such terms as "expanded consciousness" or "bliss consciousness." Traditional religious

WHAT IS MEDITATION?

meditators may seek a "union with God," "God consciousness," or a "unitative state." One hears of "killing the ego," "annihilation of the self," and "cosmic consciousness."

Do all of these terms, and many, many more, describe the same state, or at least different points on the same path? Probably they do. Yet even here there is no agreement. Some schools of meditation are of the opinion that there are many approaches to meditation, and that the individual should choose the one that suits him or her best. But other meditative schools have a very exclusive outlook, and claim that their practice alone is the only way. All others, they contend, are either ineffective, or downright dangerous and diabolical.

The problem here is that what happens during meditation is not a rational, logical, or verbal experience. If meditators agree on nothing else, they do agree that the meditation experience is highly personal and is not the sort of thing that you can talk about very effectively.

Since much of the essence of meditation cannot be directly described, devotees of the practice are very fond of telling stories which they feel illustrate aspects of the practice.

Here are two stories from vastly different cultures, which concern quite different forms of meditation. Yet both make exactly the same point.

A famous Hasidic Rabbi was to visit the Jewish community of a small Russian town. This was a great event and the men of the town spent many hours preparing the questions that they were to ask the celebrated wise man. All the men gathered in the largest available room in the town for the Rabbi's visit.

But when the Rabbi arrived, he said nothing. He just sat silently in front of the anxious group for a few moments. Then

he began to softly hum a Hasidic tune. Soon the others in the room began to hum along with him. Then he began to sing and soon everyone was singing. Then he began swaying back and forth, and finally to dance, and very soon everyone in the room was caught up in the dance.

At first the dancing was restrained and self-conscious, but as the dancing continued the men became more and more deeply involved in it. Dancing engaged the whole of their attention. After the dancing had gone on for a while, the Rabbi gradually slowed down and stopped. He looked at the group and said, "I trust I have answered all of your questions." Then he left.

In recent years the practice of Zen, a Japanese variant of Buddhism, has become increasingly popular in the U.S., particularly on college campuses. A large California university scheduled a lecture by a celebrated Zen roshi, or master, of Zen.

When the time of the lecture arrived, the hall was filled. The Zen roshi, a small Japanese man wearing a kimono, entered the room and sat down cross-legged on the stage. He explained the proper posture for Zen meditation, how the back must be kept absolutely straight, and the hands cradled in the lap, thumbs touching. Most of all, he said, one must pay attention. He said everything one could say about Zen meditation. That took about two minutes. For the remaining eighty-eight minutes of the scheduled lecture time the roshi sat in absolute stillness and silence. When the appointed time for his lecture was over, he simply got up and left the stage.

These stories are probably not literally true. Most tales told about famous rabbis, Zen roshis, Muslim dervishes, Hindu gurus, or Christain saints are not literally true—they are meant

WHAT IS MEDITATION?

to illustrate a point. In this case the point is the nonverbal, nonintellectual nature of meditation. Stories making the same point can be taken from many cultures.

Yet here I am setting out to write a whole book about a subject that practically everyone says you cannot describe. I'm certainly not the first. Hundreds, perhaps thousands, of books have been written on the subject—many of them in the last few years. The books range from long mystical autobiographies describing "spiritual journeys" to simple "how-to-do-it" books illustrated with diagrams. Recently some of these books have become enormous best sellers. Are all writers on the subject in the position of the Zen roshi, who had little to say and much time to say it in?

No, not really. We cannot adequately describe, or even approach the "experience" of the trained meditator—not because it is necessarily mysterious or difficult, but because it is not an experience that lends itself well to description. But while admitting, humbly, that no outsider can get inside of anyone else's meditation experience, there are still many useful things which can be said. There is a good deal of objective information about this most subjective and personal human experience.

Meditation has a long history and a very active present, both of which can be described. The techniques, if not the essence, of meditation can be examined. The scientific investigation of the physiological and psychological effects of meditation can be reported. And we can gain at least a measure of enlightenment from what the trained meditators have said of the experience.

In this book we are going to try and push aside some of the curtains of myth and mystery that have too often shrouded this increasingly popular subject.

2

The Range of Meditation

We know that meditation in one form or another is both extremely ancient and remarkably widespread. In this chapter we are going to try and give you some idea of the scope of this practice, particularly as it relates to the United States and the rest of the Western world today.

Where and how did meditation begin? Of course there is no way of really knowing. Harvard psychologist Gary Schwartz thinks that a need for some form of meditation may be part of our evolutionary heritage. Writing in *Psychology Today*, Schwartz has said:

"Meditative practices have existed for thousands of years. Very broadly, we may think of meditation as an act of sustained self-reflection: in this sense it is a natural act. I suspect that there is an evolutionary precedent for meditation. Primitive human societies and even certain types of apes typically spend part of each day sitting quietly, in what appears to be self-reflection. Who is to say they're not meditating?"

HINDUISM

Historically, meditation has been connected with religion. In fact, it is often regarded as a religious act itself. The oldest religion in the world today, the Hinduism of India, is also the religion in which meditation is most prominent. The Vedas, ancient religious books of the Hindus, were written in a language called Sanskrit. These books contain elaborate and detailed descriptions of many different forms of meditation and how they should be used.

The Hindu religion is difficult for Westerners to comprehend. I want to add quickly that this is not because I believe that there is such a thing as an "Oriental mind" which is somehow biologically different from the "Western mind." It is that the whole concept of the universe, and the traditions that have grown up within Hinduism for thousands of years, are very different from those that have developed in the West. There has been relatively little interchange between the two religious traditions.

Another problem in understanding Hinduism is that it is extremely unorganized, by our standards. In the West we tend to think of religions as having well-defined creeds, regular structures, and identifiable leaders with titles like bishop, minister, or rabbi. Over the centuries the Hindu religion has developed a huge and confusing number of traditions, schools, sects, and what have you. It is almost an oversimplification to call it a single religion at all.

Leadership in Hindu religion is often more personal than organizational. A teacher or guru may gather about himself a following and train disciples in his ways. But there is rarely a regular and continuing organization growing out of this personal following.

Some forms of yoga train practitioners to withstand great pain.

To some, the procession of Indian teachers with their strange titles who have come westward, wearing clothes that are unfamiliar to us and preaching their doctrines, which are even less familiar, has seemed bizarre, comical, and perhaps a bit sinister. But this movement of Hindu ideas to the West is not a phenomenon of the 1970s. It has been going on for nearly a century. As far back as 1893, Swami Vivenkananda visited the United States and founded the Vedanta society. The society still exists today. Though its membership is small, it has from time to time attracted some very prominent people, like the author Aldous Huxley.

The term "yoga" has become familiar in the West. Most of us think of a series of exotic exercises and strange postures. In Sanskrit the word connotes unity, the unity of the individual

THE RANGE OF MEDITATION

with Ultimate Reality. It is a religious concept. But there are many ways by which the spiritual objective can be approached; therefore, there are many types of yoga.

One of these types, called *Hatha Yoga*, does involve exercises and positions. It has become quite popular in the West in a nonreligious context. Many people feel that the exercises are beneficial to physical health. Yoga classes are widely available and millions of Americans have probably practiced some yoga exercises. But there is more to yoga than exercises. Meditation forms an important part of many yoga traditions. A yogi, by the way, is an individual who is trained in the practices of yoga.

Among the many forms of meditation practiced among Hindus, mantra meditation is the one that has attracted the largest number of followers in the West. The system of mantra meditation that has become so popular is called Transcendental Meditation or TM. It was introduced by Maharishi Mahesh Yogi. This system now has so many Western followers that it will be examined in greater detail in the following chapter.

There is a segment of Hinduism which relies on loud public chanting to produce a spiritual effect.

Hindu chanting has become well known to people in the West through the activities of the International Society for Krishna Consciousness or ISKCON. The group is more familiarly known as the Hare Krishnas and usually pronounced "Harry" Krishnas.

Converts to this sect can be found in most large cities in the U.S. They wear colorful Indian-style clothes and the men generally shave their heads except for a topknot, or pigtail. One of the Hare Krishnas' major activities, and one with which the public is most familiar, is chanting. A group will gather on a busy street corner and begin chanting loudly, often to the ac-

companiment of drums and cymbals. After a short while members of the group will begin dancing about and clapping. It is the sort of display that always attracts a lot of attention.

The Hare Krishna chant runs:

    HARE KRISHNA
    HARE KRISHNA
    KRISHNA KRISHNA
    HARE HARE
    HARE RAMA HARE RAMA
    RAMA RAMA
    HARE HARE

Krishna is the name given to the deity believed to be the supreme personification of the godhead. Simply repeating the sacred name is supposed to have a beneficial effect both upon those who do the chanting and those who happen to overhear the chant. That is the reason that the Hare Krishnas seek deliberately to attract attention.

The Hare Krishna movement was brought to the United States in 1965 by a seventy-year-old Indian scholar whom his followers call Prabhupada ("one at whose feet masters sit"). As of this writing Prabhupada, now eighty-two, is still alive and in firm control of his movement.

While the Maharishi has deliberately Westernized his teachings, making them easy to understand and follow, Prabhupada has remained uncompromisingly Indian and severe. As a result, practitioners of Transcendental Meditation number in the millions while Hare Krishna has attracted only a few thousand followers. This doesn't discourage Prabhupada one bit. "If you sell diamonds," he has said, "you cannot expect to have

A Hare Krishna ceremony in San Francisco

many customers. But a diamond is a diamond even if there are no buyers."

Public chanting isn't the only form of meditation in which the Hare Krishnas engage. The devotees claim that their entire life is one of meditation. If one defines meditation as concentration with a spiritual objective, then there is a good deal of merit in the claim.

In addition to the public chanting, each devotee carries out a program of personal chanting. This means repetition of the Hare Krishna mantra 1,728 times every single day. The chanting is counted on a string of 108 beads. The string must be counted through sixteen times each day. Many hours of the devotees' day is set aside for prayer and chanting, but the sixteen rounds can be completed during breaks in normal activity, such as waiting for the completion of a phone call.

The life of a member of the Hare Krishna sect is extremely ascetic and ritualized. Every act, even the most humble, is regarded as an act of devotion and, in a sense, an act of meditation. Such an attitude can also be found in other religious groups.

The wonder of the Hare Krishna movement is not that it has so few followers, but that it has any at all. Prabhupada came to the United States because he had been told to do so by his own personal guru some thirty years earlier. He arrived with little besides a suitcase full of books. He had only the remotest of contacts in the U.S. and started his movement from practically nothing.

Because of their distinctive garb and public chanting the Hare Krishnas are highly visible. The movement is also financially secure. Prabhupada's translations of Hindu scriptures sell well and the movement has become one of the largest manufacturers

of incense and other scented products. Street solicitations by devotees bring in a good deal of money every day and may be the greatest source of income. The group owns a lot of property, including an eight-story building on Manhattan's West Side and several farms and schools throughout the U. S. and in other countries as well.

The Hare Krishnas have also become highly controversial. The parents of some devotees claim that their children have been "brainwashed" by the sect. The charge is not an uncommon one to be leveled against meditation groups, and we shall return to it in more detail later.

Another Indian guru who brought his teachings and methods to the West with spectacular (if temporary) success was a teenager who was known as the Guru Maharaj Ji. He was the *Satguru*, or Perfect Master, and his followers appeared to con- consider him a divine being. During the early 1970s his Divine Light Mission attracted thousands of followers in the United States and Great Britain.

While practically every other guru or other unorthodox religious leader has, at one time or another, been accused of being a fake and a con man, these charges were particularly persistent in the case of Guru Maharaj Ji. Many of his followers lived austerely in communal centers called ashrams. The young Guru and his family lived in high style, and were driven about in a Rolls Royce.

The Guru also attracted a lot of unfavorable publicity through flashy and bizarre promotion schemes. In November, 1973, the Divine Light Mission hired the Houston Astrodome for a huge festival. It was supposed to have marked a turning point in the world's history. The stadium was rarely more than a quarter

filled, though tickets were free. The festival turned out to be a financial and public relations disaster.

Shortly thereafter the Guru married his American secretary. This led to a public squabble with other members of his family. His mother denounced him as a "playboy" and tried to throw him out of the Divine Light Mission. The movement went into rapid decline, and little has been heard from it lately—though for a short period it may have been the fastest growing religion in America.

Those full-time followers of Maharaj Ji did a great deal of meditation. Like the Hare Krishnas, they claimed that they were really in a constant state of meditation, that everything they did was basically an act of meditation. But there were more formal periods of meditations as well. Some of these meditations were of the mantra type. Others consisted of staring worshipfully at a picture of Maharaj Ji and contemplating his greatness and love. Some members of the Divine Light Mission claimed that they could remain in a state of deep meditation for hours.

Another practice of the Divine Light Mission was called *satsang*, or discourse. Members would sit around and tell one another, or any newcomers who might happen to drop in, about how wonderful it was to be a follower of Maharaj Ji. These discourses were very dull and repetitious. No one really listened to them. No one was supposed to. You were supposed to feel the "vibrations." After a while *satsang* could induce a meditative state in listeners.

Probably the most interesting feature of the Divine Light Mission practice was "Knowledge." This was supposed to be the ultimate proof of the divine status of Maharaj Ji. There was a great deal of mystery surrounding getting "Knowledge" at first, and it was very hard to get. Knowledge could only be

given by a small number of Mahatmas, individuals specially appointed by the Maharaj Ji himself. Many asked to receive Knowledge, but only a few were chosen at a time. And they were sworn never to reveal what went on in a Knowledge ceremony.

After a while, there were plenty of disenchanted followers of the Maharaj Ji around who were willing to describe the process. It turned out to be fairly simple. The Mahatma pressed upon a person's eyeballs. This produced a sensation of light—called the Divine Light. He put his fingers in the person's ears and this produced a swishing sound that was the Divine Music. He tipped the person's head back and told him to curl his tongue back along the roof of his mouth to taste the Divine Nectar. And finally he gave the initiate a "secret word," a mantra, to meditate on. It was supposed to be the sound that represented the Divine Energy of the universe. It sounded something like "ah-hah."

The devotee was instructed to train himself in these techniques and repeat them several times every day.

None of this was very startling. But there was such a buildup to the Knowledge ceremony, and it was performed with such solemnity, that many who went through it found it overpowering. They really felt they had an experience which brought them closer to an Ultimate Reality.

There was not supposed to be anything abstract or spiritual about Knowledge. It was represented as being concrete proof of the Guru Maharaj Ji powers. There are a couple of other "concrete" concepts that deserve a brief discussion.

Some who follow Eastern traditions of meditation will speak of "opening the third eye" or of how meditation will "energize the chakras." These ideas are apt to be rather startling when first encountered.

The third eye is supposed to be "the eye that sees inward."

Most traditions locate it somewhere between the two external eyes, and it is often associated with the pineal body, a small appendage of the brain. The "chakras" are supposed to be energy centers located in various parts of the body. According to most traditions there are seven of them, though the number and exact location can vary.

The pineal body does, in some ways, have a structure similar to that of an eye. But there is no scientific evidence that it is used for "seeing inward," or seeing anything else. There is no scientific evidence at all for the existence of anything like the chakras.

Many sophisticated meditators insist that such concepts as the third eye and the chakras are simply metaphors. Since meditation is highly personal, nonverbal metaphors are often used. They also point out that these concepts grew up in primitive societies. Lawrence LeShan, a psychiatrist with great sympathy for meditation, warns, "We must avoid the great seductiveness of confusing mythic language and scientific language. The myth is crucial for evaluation and communication. The fact is also crucial, but the two are not to be confused . . ."

Yet other Western students of meditation believe very deeply in the absolute reality of such things as the third eye and the chakras.

ZEN

Next to TM itself, the most popular form of meditation in the West is Zen, an outgrowth of Japanese Buddhism. Zen was first introduced into the United States in the late nineteenth century. But interest in it remained at an extremely low level, except among Japanese immigrants who learned the practice in Japan.

A Zen Buddhist monk

It wasn't until the 1950s that Zen began to attract any widespread public attention in the U.S. The practice was taken up by some California-based writers and poets who had been dubbed "the Beat Generation." Much of the "Beat's" flirtation with Zen and other forms of Oriental religion was superficial, but it did serve to bring the subject to public notice. During the early 1960s a half dozen Zen roshis, masters of Zen, came to the United States

from Japan. Regular centers where Zen meditation or *zazen* was taught began to open up around the country. Soon there were a number of Americans who had mastered the technique and were able to teach it effectively.

Today there are more than one hundred Zen groups throughout the U.S. Zen centers can be found in most major cities, and there are a number of small communes which are built around the serious, full-time practice of Zen. There are also several Zen monasteries, where students can go for a week or two of rigorous meditation called *sesshin*. During such a period, as much as fourteen hours a day may be devoted to zazen.

Of all the meditation techniques that have burgeoned in popularity in the West over the last few years, zazen is unquestionably the most austere. There are several variations available. A few Korean Zen centers have opened on the East Coast. There is a modest interest in Tibetan Buddhism, which in many ways resembles Zen. Some Americans have introduced minor modifications in the meditation technique. But basically the Zen that is seriously practiced in the United States is the same kind that is practiced in Japan.

Zazen, as the roshi are quick to remind their students, is "just sitting." But it is sitting in a very particular and often painful way.

Japanese masters usually insist on a full lotus position, that is, legs crossed with feet resting on the thighs. Orientals who are used to sitting cross-legged on the floor find the position relatively easy. For Westerners who are used to sitting in chairs, the position is extremely difficult and uncomfortable. Many start with a half-lotus; the legs are crossed but only one leg rests on the opposite thigh. Some American Zen teachers allow their students to sit in a chair, provided the meditator keeps his

Meditation was a regular part of the life of Christian monks.

ent methods of prayer for the common man. Meister Peter, the Barber was Luther's example of the common man. In order to achieve the proper mental state for some types of prayer, Luther said, one should concentrate on certain objects. He suggested the words of the Lord's Prayer, the Ten Commandments, the Psalms, or a number of the sayings of Christ or Paul. Such concentration would keep disturbing thoughts from intruding.

Organized systems of meditation are no longer common in Christianity except in monasteries or convents where time is set aside for meditation and prayer. But any form of repeated prayer, any deep concentration on a nonrational question such as the nature of God's love or the mystery of the Trinity, any prolonged staring at the cross or other religious object can be classed as meditation. Counting the beads on a rosary, in conjunction with a repeated prayer, is another meditative practice, though it is not often recognized as one.

During the Middle Ages many deeply religious Christians engaged in austerities and mortification of the flesh that might have made a modern yogi tremble. Prolonged fasting was a common religious practice, and there were hair shirts, spiked whips, and all the other instruments of self-torture. Today virtually all branches of Christianity reject these extreme practices, but at one time they were considered a mark of great spirituality.

St. John of the Cross, a sixteenth-century Spanish mystic, was an extreme ascetic. At the end of the long and painful road of asceticism St. John found the sort of paradoxical state described by so many devotees of rigorous meditation:

"In this spoliation, the soul finds its tranquility and rest. Profoundly established in the centre of its own nothingness, it can be assailed by naught that comes from below; and since it

St. John of the Cross

no longer desires anything, what comes from above cannot depress it; for 'tis desires alone are the causes of its woes."

Another Christian meditational practice has been called the path of action. In *The Little Way* of Saint Theresa of Lisieux, this celebrated sixteenth-century saint describes doing all of the small tasks of everyday life with the knowledge that each one is a part of the total harmony of the universe. These tasks were done with love, with total concentration, and with the attitude that this simple task was the most important thing at the moment.

A number of Protestant sects have adopted similar practices. They can also be found in the East. For example, aikido, the Japanese art of flower arranging is much more of a devotional activity than a method of interior decorating.

Among Protestant groups perhaps the purest form of meditation today is the Quaker meeting. In such a meeting the mem-

An orthodox Jew chants his prayers.

bers of the society sit in silent meditation until a spirit within "moves" one of them to make a statement to the assembled group. The Shakers, a celibate and communal society which flourished in America about a century ago, used ritualized, but very active, dances as part of their religious activity. That is how they got their name.

Even today many churches and chapels remain open at all

times for "prayer and meditation." Ironically the devotees of some Eastern meditational practices are advised to go into churches for their regular meditation sessions, because churches are the only public places where they can meditate undisturbed. How different are the Christians repeating their prayers, from the meditator in a nearby pew silently repeating his mantra?

A form of mantra meditation can be found in early Jewish mysticism, particularly among those who follow the Cabala, a body of Jewish mysticism. In the thirteenth century A.D., when the Rabbi Abulafia published his major works, he described a mystical system in which he methodically contemplated the letters of the Hebrew alphabet which form God's name (YHWH). The result of this contemplation was to pass into a state beyond normal consciousness.

Gershom Scholem, a modern Hebrew scholar, has written: ". . . an important part in Abulafia's system is played by the technique of breathing; now this technique has found its highest development in Indian Yoga, where it is commonly regarded as the most important instrument of mental discipline. Again, Abulafia lays down certain forms of recitation, and in particular some passages of his book, *The Light of the Intellect*, give the impression of a Judaized treatise on Yoga. The similarity even extends to some aspects of the doctrine of ecstatic vision, as preceded and brought about by these practices."

Dancing, chanting, and singing form a prominent part of the religious life of Hasidic Jews today. Most very orthodox Jews also engage in a practice called *dovening*—a ritual rocking back and forth while reading and rereading the Torah.

In the world of Islam there is a mystical tradition called Sufism. The best known of the Sufis are the so-called "whirling dervishes," holy men who can put themselves in a transcen-

Muslim mystics called whirling dervishes put themselves into a trance-like state by dancing.

dental state by dancing about in a whirling motion for hours. When Westerners first encountered the whirling dervishes they were struck with a kind of horrified fascination. The practice seemed utterly strange and primitive, and it completely obscured the rich mystical tradition which lay behind it, and the fact that not all Sufis are whirling dervishes.

Sufism has been little known in the West until comparatively recently. It is now making modest headway among those groups which have an interest in Eastern religions and mysticism. What many find so attractive about the Sufi way is that it is non-doctrinaire. One need not whirl, or chant, or even be a Muslim to be a Sufi.

Current Western interest in Sufism has been sparked primarily by the work of Idries Shah, who has translated many traditional Sufi teaching tales into English. Like most mystical

disciplines, Sufism cannot be approached directly, but is most often explained in tales like this one from Shah's *Thinkers of the East*:

Anis was asked, "What is Sufism?"

He said, "Sufism is that which succeeds in bringing to man the High Knowledge."

"But if I apply the traditional methods handed down by the masters, is that not Sufism?"

"It is not Sufism if it does not perform its function for you. A cloak is no longer a cloak if it does not keep a man warm."

"So Sufism does change?"

"People change and needs change. So what was Sufism once is Sufism no more.

"Sufism," continued Anis, "is the external face of internal knowledge, known as High Knowledge. The inner factor does not change. The whole work, therefore, is the High Knowledge, plus capacity, which produces method. What you are pleased to call Sufism is merely the record of past method."

A problem with this tolerant attitude is that practically anyone who is doing anything vaguely related to the problem of human consciousness and self-realization can call himself a Sufi. Since the word has become popular over the last few years, an awful lot of people have done just that.

Modern Developments

Of modern innovators in mysticism, one of the most influential, and strangest, was Gurdjieff. George Ivanovitch Gurdjieff was a Greek born in Russia near the Persian border in about 1877. A great deal about Gurdjieff's early life, and the influences upon his work, is shrouded in mystery, most of it

The Muslim mystical tradition known as Sufism has become increasingly popular in the West.

deliberately created by Gurdjieff himself. After traveling around, primarily in the Middle East and the Orient, Gurdjieff returned to Russia and collected a group of disciples. When the Russian Revolution broke out, Gurdjieff found himself caught between opposing forces in a land that was being torn apart. So he left for the more peaceful provinces of Western Europe, and spent most of the rest of his life in Paris. He died there in 1949.

Gurdjieff was an imposing figure, with a shaven head and fierce mustache. He was the perfect picture of a Tartar. He was a showman and undoubtedly something of a charlatan as well. He liked money and what it could buy. His mansion outside of Paris was sumptuous. He made his money from the rich people who gathered about him to be "enlightened," or cured of a variety of ailments. "Fleecing the sheep," he used to call it. But Gurdjieff also attracted a nucleus of really talented followers, who found a great deal in his work, and have kept his name and teachings very much alive to this day.

The features about Gurdjieff that attracted the most attention were the dances. These were probably derived from dervish dances, though no one is really sure. Gurdjieff had once directed a dance troupe in Moscow. Gurdjieff taught his followers that these elaborate, difficult, and exhausting dances were a way to inner knowledge. The dances were performed with total concentration. When this idea first was presented in the United States in the 1930s it seemed quite startling. A "dance recital" by some of Gurdjieff's students left the uninitiated audience puzzled and angry.

Small groups and communities that try to follow Gurdjieff's teachings exist throughout the world. But his influence cannot be judged only by the number of acknowledged followers. Dur-

ing the 1940s a young Bolivian named Oskar Ichazo joined a Gurdjieff group in Buenos Aires. He was trying to find some relief from the violent and inexplicable attacks which had afflicted him since early childhood. Gurdjieff's teachings had a powerful influence on his life, though he never became a disciple. Rather, they stimulated Oskar (as he is usually called) to look into other forms of mystic training—Yoga, Sufism, Zen among them.

Oskar finally formed his own group called Arica, which in recent years has been expanding in the United States. Arica's most notable convert to date is John Lilly, an M.D. and research scientist who first became famous for his work on communicating with dolphins.

Arica isn't easy. Training is expensive and physically taxing. It isn't the sort of thing that you can start in your spare time. The first training course is forty days, followed by advanced programs for graduates. Arica meditation can include practically anything—slow motion walking, chanting, dancing, carrying a heavy rock—whatever, in Oskar Ichazo's opinion, seems to help the development of consciousness. Oskar insists that his methods are very scientific, and that the various exercises have been proved, by experience, to be successful.

Here is a typical Arica exercise as described by George Goodman who writes under the name Adam Smith:

"One of the exercises—you could call it a meditation—went like this. You get a rock. (Some people got very pretty rocks, since they were going to be doing this exercise six days a week, four hours a day.) Class exercise. You put your rock on the floor in front of you; you can sit on a pillow. You put your consciousness in the rock. I was confused. How do you do that?

Now take a breath, pick up the rock, hold your breath, and move the rock in a circle in front of you. Your eyes are shut. And while you move the rock, you think, *Om namo naraya naya*, which you can spot immediately as a Sanskrit mantram. Then you exhale and put the rock down, take another breath, and do the same thing left-handed, two repetitions of the mantram per circle of the rock per breath. That's the beginning; it goes on. The last motion—same mantram going—is to circle your head with the rock, and visualize a white light making the same circle inside your head."

Then you start the exercise all over again. It goes on for four hours. Arica isn't easy, and isn't for everyone.

Is it for anyone? Arica is very controversial. In the past it has been rather secretive, and clearly under the total control of founder Oskar Ichazo himself. One critic called Arica "spiritual fascism." Oskar himself admits that the program can be tough, once describing it as "a complex mixture of ashram, monastery and boot camp." But instead of "spiritual fascism," Oskar describes his organization as "democratic mysticism."

Late in 1976, Oskar felt that Arica was on the verge of a major expansion. "We are finished with the groundwork and have a blueprint for the whole future structure," he told an interviewer. "We will now go outside and face the public. And, although ours is quite an elaborate system which makes considerable demands on the individual, we have developed guidelines of sufficient clarity to the general public. This has been based on a lot of testing on exercises at different levels. When we are dealing with such practices as meditations that require several hours we must engage in weeks of preparations so that the final results will be a true accomplishment for each person."

Another modern group that deserves a mention is Subud. Subud is the creation of an Indonesian Muslim named Mohammed Subuh, or Bapack, as he is called by his followers. The central act of Subud is "an experience" called Latihan. Members of Subud are very reluctant to describe this experience, mainly because they believe that words are of little value, and because everyone experiences Latihan differently.

Twice a week or so Subud members gather in a special room. They stand around and wait for "something" to happen. For some people nothing happens, and after a while they get bored and go away. Others, however, feel that they are being put in touch with "higher energies," that is, the Latihan.

According to Subud literature, "During the Latihan, the mind, the heart, the will, and the desires are each rendered more or less inactive. . ." In such a state of submission, the individual is "open" to higher forces which guide one though a process of purification, and yet one is both fully conscious and in control of whether one wishes to continue or not.

Sometimes during Latihan individuals will scream or jump around or fall to the floor. But the Latihans have become considerably quieter since Subud was first introduced to the West in 1957. Some followers of Subud report that Latihan has produced highly beneficial changes in their daily life, a claim often made for more popular meditational practices.

Dr. Herbert Benson, who has studied meditation closely, also notes, "We see the same sort of things [meditation] in the writings of the so-called 'nature mystics.' Wordsworth believed that anyone could deliberately induce a 'happy stillness of the mind' through a deliberate relaxation of the will. Tennyson, as his son later revealed, was able to induce altered states of consciousness through a steady repetition of his own name."

THE RANGE OF MEDITATION

This is far from a complete survey of human meditational practices. But it should give you some idea of the reach of such practices. In one way or another they are found in practically every culture, at every point in history. The names are different, the practices often look different, but the aims and results appear to be very similar.

Now let's take a closer look at TM, the fastest-growing form of meditation in the West today.

3

TM—The Big One

Transcendental Meditation, or TM, has been called the McDonald's of meditation.

That description is not an entirely friendly one. But it isn't altogether an inaccurate description either.

First, there is the tremendous popularity of TM. The Gallup survey mentioned at the beginning of this book found that 4 percent of their sample practiced Transcendental Meditation. A projection from that sample would indicate that some six million Americans were engaged in the practice of TM in mid-1976.

That number is far higher than even the most devoted supporters of TM had estimated. Their estimates for the same period run from three-quarters of a million to one million. It may well be that many of those who told the Gallup pollsters that they were practicing TM were really doing some other form of meditation, and simply responded with the most familiar term. Confusion in this area is common, much to the distress of the regular practitioners of TM.

TM—THE BIG ONE

TM is a registered trademark, but anyone can use the term Transcendental Meditation and many have. A number of individuals and groups are trading on the popularity of TM, by advertising that they teach Transcendental Meditation. Members of the TM establishment, however, insist that there is one, and only one, way in which the true practice of Transcendental Meditation can be learned. It cannot be learned from a book, nor can anyone who has not been trained and authorized by the TM hierarchy teach the practice. All other practices, they say, are weak and ineffective imitations.

Whatever the true number of real TM practitioners, there can be no disputing that it is far and away the largest of the newly introduced meditational practices. Much of the current popularity of meditation is a direct result of the enormous popularity and acceptance gained by TM. Many large bookstores now have special sections set aside for books on meditation. The majority of these are about TM, and it is only the TM books that become best sellers.

TM centers exist in all large U.S. cities, and near major college campuses where there is always a great interest in unorthodox or unusual practices. But they can be found in many small cities and towns as well. And there is hardly an area in the country, no matter how rural and remote, which has not been visited at least once by TMers offering free introductory lectures at a local motel or meeting hall.

Another comparison between the popular fast-food chain and TM is the standardization of the product. Whether one learns TM in New York City or Sioux City, Iowa, the instruction is absolutely the same, allowing for only minor variations due to differing personalities of the instructors. This is not necessarily a criticism of the practice. Those within TM freely admit that

their teachings are standardized. Teachers and checkers (whose job it is to make sure that the person is carrying out TM properly) have regular lists which they consult as to procedure. They are told to say "we" or "ours" rather than "you," "yours" or "I." Questions, answers, and speeches are all laid out beforehand; there is little room for individuality or spontaneity. TM is easy to learn, say its followers, but there is only one way to learn it.

One final comparison between TM and the fast-food chain, both the process and the product are specifically tailored to appeal to modern American tastes, and to fit into the rushed pace of modern American life. TM might well echo the familiar McDonald's slogan, "You deserve a break today." Once again, that is not necessarily a criticism. Members of the TM hierarchy admit, indeed advertise, the fact that TM is specifically tailored to modern life.

But if TM is consciously modern, its origins are ancient. TM is a form of mantra meditation based on the Vedas, the extremely ancient holy books of Hinduism. The man who modernized the practice is not some well-tailored, high-powered Madison Avenue promoter. He is a bearded Indian, who wears traditional garb and got his training meditating in a cave in the Himalayas. His name is Maharishi Mahesh Yogi. Maharishi is an honorary title meaning, roughly, "great sage." He is generally referred to as the Maharishi or simply Maharishi. Mahesh is his name and Yogi designates one dedicated to a particular belief.

The Maharishi was born something over sixty years ago in Central India, the son of a local tax official. He went to Allahabad University where he studied physics. He also worked in a factory in Jubbulpore, but then decided on spiritual pursuits

and took up a study of the classics of the Hindu religion.

The Maharishi came under the influence of Swami Brahmanand Saraswati and for thirteen years was his disciple. The Swami is also known as Guru Dev, or Divine Teacher, and, while long dead, is still a revered figure in the TM movement. At the very beginning of TM training the novice brings a small offering which is placed in front of a picture of Guru Dev.

The Maharishi spent two years as a monk in a cave in the Himalayas, and then set out on his mission, which he asserts was given him by Guru Dev. The mission was no small one; it was nothing less than transformation of the entire world through Transcendental Meditation. Though TM today is hardly sweeping the world, the Maharishi has succeeded astonishingly well, considering that he started with nothing, and not so very long ago either.

The Maharishi began his mission in the Indian state of Madras in December, 1967. The following year he made his first world tour. A meeting of the movement's international leaders in Sequoia National Park, California, in 1969 was small and attracted little attention from press or public.

Up to this point the Maharishi was generally identified as the leader of "the Hindu Order of Shankar Acharya." Transcendental Meditation had not yet dominated the movement. At exactly what point, and why the Maharishi decided to change the name and thrust of his teachings from a religious movement to what is now generally called a technique for developing human potential, is not clear. But the change turned out to be a highly important one.

In the late 1960s the Maharishi was giving lectures in London's Picadilly Hotel. Among those who attended the lectures and were impressed by what they heard were the Beatles, then

at the height of their popularity. The Beatles had been involved with psychoactive drugs, had become disenchanted with them, and were looking for new methods of "expanding their consciousness." Eastern religions were one of these methods. In that respect the Beatles were not unlike many of their young admirers of the 1960s.

The Beatles became followers of Maharishi, even journeying with him to India. The association with the world-famous rock group gained the Maharishi considerable fame, and probably a great deal of money. It lasted for about a year, and when the Beatles left, they had bitter things to say about the amount of money the Maharishi was getting. Later, other show business celebrities were attracted to the Maharishi's movement, the best known being actress Mia Farrow and the singing group, the Beach Boys.

Still, the abrupt and disagreeable departure of the Beatles cost the TM movement dearly in terms of publicity. The press stopped paying particular attention to the Maharishi. Without the Beatles he was just another Eastern guru, or so it appeared to many.

While the Maharishi dropped out of the spotlight for a time, his movement continued to grow steadily. TM became particularly popular in California, which is often fertile ground for new ideas and movements.

Many meditation disciplines resist scientific probing. They say that science is too restrictive, or that it has nothing to do with what they are doing. Some simply resent science generally, while others may fear that it will expose something about them. But TM welcomed and embraced the idea of science, and invited scientific investigation. Moreover, by the early 1970s, there were enough people in America trained in the technique

Maharishi Mahesh Yogi, founder of the TM movement

of TM for adequate large-scale studies to be conducted.

Robert Keith Wallace was one of many California students who was attracted to TM. He had become a dedicated meditator and felt that the technique had a great deal to offer. For his Ph.D. thesis in physiology Wallace proposed a study to find out just what happened to a person's body during meditation. Twenty-seven trained TM meditators were wired up to a variety of instruments. These instruments checked temperature, blood pressure, heart rate, brain waves, and skin resistance (a measure of relaxation). Through a catheter in the arm the chemical content of the subject's blood was constantly measured during the meditation period.

Though all of this hardware would hardly seem conducive to the serenity necessary for meditation, the instruments were painless, and were kept hidden behind a screen during the test. No one seemed to be bothered by them.

The results from the meditators were compared with measurements taken from a similar group of people who were not meditating, but just sitting quietly. Wallace's work was done in cooperation with Herbert Benson, a cardiologist and assistant professor of medicine at the Harvard Medical School. The results were striking. The meditators showed dramatic increases in skin resistance, decreases in the level of blood lactate, oxygen consumption, respiration, and a host of other physiological changes which indicated that the meditators were in a state of profound rest, a "general quiescence of the nervous system." Meditators were far more relaxed than the subjects who were just sitting. The paper concluded that TM produced a distinctly different state of consciousness and that the procedure "may have practical applications."

The Benson-Wallace paper was printed in *Science*, the offi-

cial publication of the American Association for the Advancement of Science, and one of the most prestigious scientific journals in the world. Reports of the Benson-Wallace study appeared in a number of other authoritative scientific publications, and began to spread to the general press as well.

The effect of this initial study was monumental as far as TM was concerned. There had long been a suspicion, on the part of those skeptical of meditation, that there was nothing special about the meditative state. To the casual observer, there was no difference between a person sitting quietly with his eyes closed, and a person sitting quietly with his eyes closed and meditating. The Benson-Wallace study showed that there was a big difference. The meditator was more relaxed. The meditator was in some ways even more relaxed than a person who was asleep—a rather surprising finding, since the meditator was very definitely awake.

While a certain quietness of mind has been a stated goal of many meditative disciplines, physical relaxation is not (though many Eastern philosophies do not draw a sharp distinction between mind and body). Yet relaxation is what the scientific study had indicated that TM produced, and relaxation is something much sought after in the hurried modern world.

Stress and tension of one sort or another have been implicated in a wide variety of diseases. Some medical men believe that stress plays a part in virtually all human ailments. Not only does lowering stress and reducing tension reduce the chance of illness, it also simply makes one feel better and work better. Yet practically every observer of modern life contends that we are put under a great deal of stress daily, and that we do not know how to cope with it properly. As a result, many of us are unhappy and unwell. TM seemed to promise an easy and effective

way of coping with the stress and tension without drugs or drastic changes in lifestyle. Some doctors even began recommending meditation to their anxious patients.

This sort of publicity sent thousands flocking to TM lectures and enrolling in TM courses. While in the past those who took up meditation were generally spiritual seekers, many, probably most of those who came to TM, were a different sort—they were trying to relax, improve their health, quiet their anxieties, and perhaps improve their on-the-job performance. The same sort of thing had once happened to yoga. For the Hindu, yoga is part of a religious life; for most Americans taking yoga classes at the local YMCA, it is a way of improving muscle tone or gaining other purely physical benefits.

But whatever their motives, this new breed of meditator was welcomed by TM. "Let them come," the Maharishi's devoted followers seemed to say. "They will reduce their stress, but other spiritual benefits will follow, even if they are unlooked for."

Major General Franklin M. Davis, commandant of the Army War College, took up meditation, because it "helped me in dealing with people, improved my disposition, and brought my blood pressure down."

Writer Maggie Scarf who took up TM, and liked it, wrote of her experiences in *The New York Times Magazine*. "My only problem with TM," she said, "is trying to explain it to friends and acquaintances. Those of more mystical and religious inclination insist that I cannot divorce meditation from its theological and metaphysical origins. They look shocked when I reply that to me it's no more than a terrific aspirin, a wonderful kind of bromide. My more rationalist, outer-reality-oriented friends seem to think, on the other hand, that I've adopted some strange

set of beliefs and now imagine myself experiencing 'physiological reactions' for that reason."

Celebrities again took up the practice. The entire cast of the TV series "The Waltons" was said to meditate regularly. But the biggest inroads were made among sports figures, not usually considered among the more spiritually oriented members of our society.

Joe Namath was so enthusiastic about TM that an endorsement from him is included in a TM advertising brochure.

"I took the Transcendental Meditation course because I felt like I wasn't doing anything for myself, for the growth of my system. I was wasting time. I wasn't reading. I wasn't doing anything. I wasn't really growing. So I started meditating because of the effects it has on your body and your mind, and it's done a great deal for me. It's made me feel like I am helping myself, and through that I can get along with other people and maybe help them a little more with different situations or problems. The main thing, though, I feel like it's helping me, and that in itself has done much for my whole togetherness. I feel like I'm not wasting myself, that I am helping my mind and my body live life in the right way. And I've enjoyed it and I'm going to keep on enjoying it."

Other star athletes like Willie Stargell and Jim Lonborg, as well as a host of lesser lights, have also endorsed the TM program.

All supporters of TM stress that it is extremely easy to learn, and it is. Everyone who wishes to enter a TM program is required to attend two free introductory lectures. The requirement is absolute, even if one already knows a great deal about TM and learns nothing new at the lectures.

The lectures are given by a pair of teachers, often quite

young. The first of the lectures, called "A Vision of Possibilities," outlines, in a general sort of way, what TM is supposed to do for you, how natural it is, and how it will allow you to reach your full potential as well as relaxing you. It also hints at some broader social aims. The Maharashi has always claimed that if enough people took up TM, wars would cease, corruption would end, and the world would be transformed, for mankind would have been transformed. In the first introductory lecture, studies are cited which purport to show that in a few areas where there is a large percentage of meditators, crime rates have begun to go down.

The second lecture goes into the principles of the TM technique, again in a general sort of way. If you wish to go further you have a brief personal interview with a TM teacher. The teacher tells you, among other things, that you are supposed to keep your mantra secret, and that if you don't it will ruin the whole process—but no pledges of secrecy are required. A fee, however, is required for further instruction. At the time of this writing it is $125 for adults, $65 for college students, $55 for high school students, and $35 for junior high school students. Children under ten are charged two weeks allowance. An entire family can take the course for $200. TM fees have been rising gradually over the years.

The potential student is given a brief personal questionnaire to fill out, listing age, occupation, address, and so on. Then an appointment is made for the beginning of instruction. The student is told that if he uses drugs he should not use them for at least two weeks before instruction, and that he should not eat a heavy meal just before the session. Then he is asked to bring an offering of six fresh-cut flowers, some fruit, and a white handkerchief to the session. While much of the introduc-

tion to TM is made to sound very scientific, that particular request seems strange and mysterious. It often disconcerts people.

On the appointed day the novice arrives for his instruction and is ushered into a darkened room, decorated with flowers, bowls of fruit, smelling of incense and lighted by a few candles. Pictures of Maharishi and Guru Dev are on the wall. The novice is told that his offerings are symbolic, the flower of life, the fruit the seed of life, and the white handkerchief, the cleansing of the spirit.

The teacher then chants a ceremony, or *puja*, which is in Sanskrit. The novice naturally understands nothing of this, but is told that it is the ceremony of initiation, thanking the masters of the Vedic tradition for having preserved the technique of Transcendental Meditation and for sharing it. Critics of TM claim that this ceremony is, in fact, the traditional token of submission of a student to his guru, or teacher.

The final syllables of the *puja* are the "secret mantra" which is supposed to have been specially chosen for that particular student.

There is probably no part of the entire TM program that arouses more curiosity and controversy than this "secret mantra." How, one wonders, can a special mantra be chosen to fit an individual's personal character when the teacher has only met that individual for a half hour, and has requested only the most obvious information on a questionnaire? TM teachers absolutely refuse to discuss the process of mantra selection.

Does every TMer have an individual one-of-a-kind mantra? Considering the number of people who have taken up TM, that idea seems impossible. How many mantras are there then? The Maharishi, and others in the organization, don't like that question, and will not answer it directly. According to *Time* mag-

azine, however, there are only seventeen mantras, and these are used over and over again. TM officials will neither confirm, nor flatly deny the *Time* assertion.

Many people who have taken up TM, and been disappointed with it—or who just plain can't keep a secret—have revealed their mantras. The pseudonymous Adam Smith wrote in *Powers of the Mind* that the mantra given to him was *Shiam*. He was disappointed because it didn't sound like Sanskrit.

After being given the mantra, the instructor tells the student to close his eyes and begin repeating the word over and over to himself until it is firmly fixed in his mind. If thoughts come, let them come but keep the mantra going.

The student is told that he should find a comfortable, relatively quiet, place and meditate for fifteen to twenty minutes twice a day—no more and no less. It is recommended that meditation not take place directly after a meal because digestion might interfere with the process. Other than that, there are few rules or restrictions.

After the individual instruction there are three more group sessions, which are concerned primarily with what TMers call "checking." This is asking questions to find out if the meditation is being carried out properly, and discussing any problems that may arise.

The questions asked by the checkers are usually simple. "How do you feel after you meditated?" "Do you ever lose track of your mantra?"

Some people have reported serious, even violent, reactions to beginning meditation. There have been stories of anxiety attacks, dizziness, nausea, even vomiting after initial meditation sessions. But the vast majority experience no serious reactions. It is, as TM advertises, easy and natural.

Many people have trouble finding the time and place for meditation. It is a lot more difficult than you might imagine for busy people to find two quiet and undisturbed periods during the day. Some people have resorted to locking themselves in the bathroom for meditation. Others meditate on a train or bus while commuting to work. Fellow travelers think they are napping.

There are no solid figures on TM dropouts. The TM organization is reluctant to discuss dropouts, for TM is supposed to be so easy that anyone can do it, and dropouts represent a failure of the system. The Stanford Research Institute, which conducted several studies on TM, found that about 50 percent of their meditating subjects had given up the practice within the first year. Leon S. Otis of SRI called the fact that 50 percent stayed with the practice "fairly remarkable," and indeed it is very high when compared to other self-improvement techniques where dropout rates average 80 percent and above. Still, a 50 percent dropout rate indicates that TM is not for everyone.

The SRI study found that people who were extremely anxious or depressed usually gave up on TM because they felt it didn't do enough for them, or they just couldn't sit still for two twenty-minute periods. People who were happy and had little anxiety felt they didn't need TM, so they gave it up. It was the middle group, people who were well integrated but anxious, who tended to stick with the program.

Most people who enter the TM program do so with limited aims. When they finish, they do their two sessions of meditation a day, and that is the end of it. A small number, however, go further. They become lecturers, checkers, or teachers, or otherwise enter the complicated and growing organization that the Maharishi has set up to further his World Plan of bringing enlightenment and peace through meditation.

MEDITATION: WHAT IT CAN DO FOR YOU

Few casual meditators have much interest in the Maharishi's mysticism either. Evidence for this can be found in the fact that a book about TM which emphasized the relaxation aspect and was filled with scientific validation was on the best-seller list for twenty-five weeks. The Maharishi's own book, which contains such phrases as "Contemplation on the inner-value of life eventually reveals to the aspirant that the ever-changing world is based on a never-changing element of no-form and no-phenomenon," was not nearly as popular. Most meditators do not really care about the "inner-value of life"; they are looking for Maggie Scarf's "terrific aspirin."

It was inevitable that any practice that has grown as large as TM would attract critics. TM has its share, perhaps more than its share.

Quite possibly the harshest critics are the members and leaders of other Eastern spiritual disciplines. They believe that TM has simplified ancient meditation practices to the point of meaninglessness. In order to achieve great spiritual benefits, they assert, an individual must do a great deal of spiritual hard work. There is no easy way, as TM promises.

While TM has made many followers in the United States and other Western countries, the Maharishi is not well known in his own country and has only a few thousand followers there. He has also been severely criticized by a number of Hindu spiritual leaders.

Bhagwan Shree Rajneesh, leader of the Sannyas International Movement, has said of the TM mantra, "Their mantra is useful if you want to go to sleep and can't. Recite it long enough and you will fall asleep, from boredom."

Prabhupada, leader of the Hare Krishnas, is even more severe. He told an interviewer:

"They [followers of TM] do not know what real meditation is. Their meditation is simply a farce, another cheating process by the so-called swamis and yogis . . . So everyone is talking about meditation, but no one knows what meditation is. These bluffers use the word meditation, but they do not know the proper subject for meditation. They're simply talking bogus propaganda. . . . Real meditation means to achieve a state in which the mind is saturated by God consciousness."

Krishnamurti, an Indian who has taught in the West for many years and is widely respected, is scornful of all mantra meditation techniques. "By repeating Amen or Om or Coca-Cola indefinitely you obviously have a certain experience because by repetition the mind becomes quiet. . .it is one of the favorite gambits of some teachers of meditation to insist on their pupils learning concentration, that is, fixing the mind on one thought and driving out all other thoughts. This is a most stupid, ugly thing, which any schoolboy can do because he is forced to."

So it appears that the Maharishi has a lot of enemies among those who one might think were his natural allies. But one might just set this down to jealousy and bickering among competing gurus. The Maharishi makes few public statements about such critics.

Another charge that has been made is that Maharishi is nothing more than a religious racketeer, who has made a fortune fleecing his gullible followers. It is quite true that TM is now a multimillion dollar industry with extensive real estate holdings in the U.S. and abroad. This vast enterprise is under the direct control of the Maharishi. The Maharishi often travels by private jet and is chauffeured about in a Rolls Royce.

But aside from these rather opulent travel arrangements, which might well be essential to the leader of such a vast and

far-flung organization, there is no evidence that the Maharishi lives the life of a jet-setter. He dresses and eats simply, as he always did. The money made by TM appears to go back into expanding the movement, rather than into the Maharishi's personal bank account. It must also be noted that charges of financial fraud are almost always leveled against leaders of unorthodox movements by their enemies.

Most significant is that the fees charged by TM are not all that high. There are no hidden costs, no extra fees to be paid for the revelation of greater secrets or deeper mysteries. Most of those who go through the TM course feel that they have received good value for their money.

Maggie Scarf was somewhat embarrassed when she told a friend that she had probably paid $125 for a "nonsense word."

"But to my surprise my questioner shook her head in disagreement. 'Not at all; I think it's a bargain. Look at me. I've been in analysis four days a week at $50 a time, for the past year. And my therapist still hasn't come up with my nonsense word!' "

Some profess to find something sinister in the Maharishi's plan to transform the world. But practically all religions and philosophies that believe that they are in possession of a great truth wish to spread the word to the entire world, and most believe that the world will be transformed by this truth. In that respect, TM is no different.

Which brings up another problem in connection with TM. Is it a religion? The TM organization insists that it is not. Their official literature calls TM "a simple technique to develop in a spontaneous way the full potential of the individual." The literature goes on to insist that "No belief or faith is required for the practice to work. There are no moral tenents involved: the

TM—THE BIG ONE

TM program is not a religion or a philosophy, and there is no conflict with one's existing affiliations."

It is certainly true that thousands upon thousands of regular practicing Protestants, Catholics, and Jews have taken up TM and have continued to attend to their regular religious practices without the slightest feeling of conflict. Some Western religious leaders have endorsed TM, most of them regarding it as a relaxing technique not directly related to religion.

But not everyone has taken such a view. From time to time TM courses have been taught in public schools. The federal government has even funded some studies on the effectiveness of TM teaching in schools. One of the claims often made by TM is that meditation can improve school work. Early in 1976 a coalition of fundamentalist clergymen, civil libertarians, and concerned parents filed suit in New Jersey to stop the teaching of TM in public schools. The claim was that such teaching violated the separation of church and state because TM was a "subtly disguised form of Hinduism." The lawyer representing the group has stated that "TM is a religion or a religious exercise" and "its presence in school constitutes a flagrant violation of the constitutional separation of church and state."

The TM organization denies that their practice is a religion and is fighting the suit. At the time of this writing there has been no resolution to the case and no way of predicting which way it may go. The case may be in the courts for years. But the challenge is just one more indication of the increasing attacks upon TM.

Is TM or any other form of meditation a religious exercise? I suppose that depends upon one's definition of religion. But it is interesting to note that some opponents of the Supreme Court's ban on prayer in public schools have tried to get around it by

proposing a period of "silent meditation." It is widely acknowledged that this is simply a device by which a form of prayer can be reintroduced into the schools. One wonders how the backers of such a proposal would react if the students used the period to repeat their Sanskrit mantra or mutter Hare Krishna.

Another criticism of TM is that some of its strange and exotic ideas are hidden behind a soothing flow of modern but meaningless rhetoric. Take the choice of a mantra, for example. TM teachers rarely come to grips, in public, with the question of why an ancient Sanskrit mantra is supposed to be better for meditation than a word like God, or Krishnamurti's Coca-Cola. The Maharishi has written that particular words have vibrations which are consistent with certain personalities. He also says that words set up vibrations in the atmosphere and that "vibrations of good quality [are necessary] for an influence of harmony and happiness, it is also necessary for the quality of the vibration to correspond to that of the individual."

Talk of "vibrations" of one sort or another is very common in modern mysticism. Such notions have even crept into everyday language; we may speak of feeling "good vibrations" or "good vibes." It sounds rather scientific, but it isn't. While it is quite true that sound waves do set up vibrations, there is not a scrap of evidence to indicate that there are such things as individual vibrations, or that certain sound wave vibrations are better than others. The Maharishi is simply restating some ancient beliefs in modern-sounding language. Yet this is surely the rationale behind the entire idea of a "secret mantra." "Ancient wisdom" is not the same as "scientific proof," though TM supporters do not always make or perhaps even know the difference.

But probably the most telling criticism of TM is that it has simply been oversold. The Maharishi preaches, and his follow-

ers devoutly and sincerely believe, that TM provides an answer not only to all personal problems, but to all world problems as well.

TMers tend to regard much of the criticism directed against them as unfair and carping. It is an emotional matter with many, for they feel that they owe their sanity and even their lives to this simple technique of mantra meditation.

Dr. Harold Bloomfield's book on TM contains a number of dramatic accounts.

Joan was a chronic insomniac, who suffered horribly from nervous tension before taking up TM.

"The TM program has opened up new horizons in my life. Prior to beginning the TM program I felt like I was on a treadmill. The strain was becoming unbearable, and I was on the verge of a nervous breakdown. Since meditating I gradually learned to be more at ease with myself and with the situations in my life. It's not so much that my life situation has changed, but my view of these situations. I attribute a lot of these changes to the deep calm that I've obtained from meditation."

An even more dramatic account comes from a middle-aged woman called Lisa who had actually been hospitalized for depression following a suicide attempt. She described her first meditation:

"It was wonderful. I never experienced anything quite like it. I now understand what it means to be fully relaxed and what it means to be able to look at the world through clear eyes instead of seeing it as so tension filled all the time. I felt better the rest of that day than I have felt in years. If meditation can help me to eventually be like that most of the time, I couldn't ask for more. No medication that I've taken, and I've taken lots, helped me to feel that way.

MEDITATION: WHAT IT CAN DO FOR YOU

"I find that meditating twice daily helps me to sleep better, helps me to get out of bed in the morning and start the day. Before I started meditating, I frequently used to lay around in bed all day. I am now better able to handle suicidal impulses when I have them, and have much more hope than I did before. Don't let me make it sound, however, like it made my life all better, because it hasn't. I still find it hard to get along with other people and can't find a job, but just having meditated for six weeks I feel that it's helped me to sleep better, be less depressed, and less anxious. I'm going to stick with it because it is something I can do for myself to cope better."

In a scientific sense, anecdotal evidence like this proves very little, and perhaps we have become a little cynical about testimonials, for we have heard so many of them. But it is quite impossible to talk to a large number of TMers without being impressed by their devotion and gratitude to the practice. Their testimony cannot be ignored.

TMers have another card to play. They say that in addition to individual testimony they have hard scientific validation for their claims. But do they? That is a subject we will explore in the next chapter.

4

TM vs. RR

The most serious challenge to TM has come from a man who at first appeared to be one of the movement's greatest benefactors. That man is Harvard cardiologist Herbert Benson. It was Dr. Benson, along with Robert Keith Wallace, who first prepared the report which brought TM an unprecedented amount of attention and scientific respectability.

Yet from the beginning Benson and Wallace had been very different in their attitudes toward the Maharishi's system. Wallace was a meditator who sought to validate a procedure to which he was already deeply committed. He went on to become an important figure in the international TM organization.

Benson had never meditated, did not take up meditation after the study, and never intends to. He has said that practicing meditation might reduce his scientific objectivity about the subject. Benson had never been interested in TM *per se*. He was interested in TM as an effective technique for reducing stress, and promoting relaxation. The mystical claims and global goals of TM were of little concern to him.

MEDITATION: WHAT IT CAN DO FOR YOU

Herbert Benson is one of those physicians who is convinced that the daily stress of modern life leads to many illnesses, particularly high blood pressure or hypertension. He is currently director of the Hypertension Section of Boston's Beth Israel Hospital.

Hypertension is today's "hot" disease—by that I mean there is a great deal of medical attention being paid to it. At one time only extremely high blood pressure was considered dangerous. Now researchers find that even those with moderately elevated levels of blood pressure have a greater incidence of stroke, heart attacks, kidney failure, and other damaging and deadly diseases. Somewhere between one-seventh and one-third of all adults suffer from some form of hypertension.

Most medical men also feel that stress plays a part in high blood pressure, but no one is quite sure how. What is known is that man, like all other higher animals, possesses an innate fight or flight response. When faced with a threat an animal's body, and our own, "gears up," ready to do battle or run, whichever the situation demands. A number of measurable changes take place within the body at this time, among them a rise in blood pressure and an increase in heart rate. The fight or flight response is automatic, and in appropriate situations it is extremely useful.

"But," says Benson, "the response is not used as it was intended—that is, in preparation for running or fighting with an enemy. Today, it is often brought on by situations that require behavioral adjustments, and when not used appropriately, which is most of the time, the fight or flight response repeatedly elicited may ultimately lead to the dire diseases of heart attack and stroke."

If there is an automatic fight or flight response, was there

also the opposite, an automatic response to a situation which makes us relax? Benson thought that there was. With TM he thought he had found a method of eliciting this response. The physiological reactions produced during meditation were almost the exact opposite of those produced during the excitement of the fight or flight response. If the fight or flight response could be harmful to modern man, then the relaxation response (sometimes called RR) could be helpful.

But was TM the only way of triggering this response? Benson noted that there was an enormous number of similar practices throughout the world. It seemed to the Boston doctor that there must be certain key elements common to all of these practices which could be adapted to a simple system which could be learned without secret mantras or compulsory lectures. Benson and his associates believed that they could identify the four essential elements in any meditation technique that evoked the relaxation response. These elements are:

1. A quiet environment.

2. A mental device, a word or phrase that is repeated over and over again in a particular way.

3. The adoption of a passive, "let it happen" attitude. This is the most important of all the elements in Benson's opinion.

4. A comfortable position.

Benson suggests that these four elements be practiced for ten to twenty minutes once or twice daily. It should, says Benson, "markedly enhance your well-being."

In his own studies, conducted at Beth Israel Hospital, Benson has subjects sit quietly in a comfortable position, and then relax all of their muscles, and keep them relaxed.

Like many other meditation systems, but unlike TM, Benson has his subjects concentrate on their breathing. His instructions

read, "As you breathe out, say the word 'ONE' silently to yourself. For example, breathe IN. . . . .OUT, 'ONE'; IN. . .OUT, 'ONE', etc. Breathe easily and naturally."

He tells subjects to continue the procedure for ten to twenty minutes. They may open their eyes and check the time, but should not set an alarm. Setting an alarm produces a degree of anxiety, as the subject waits for the alarm to go off. After the period is over the subject is requested to sit quietly for several more minutes, at first with the eyes closed and later with the eyes open.

Most important, Benson urges his subjects not to worry about whether they are achieving levels of deep relaxation or not. Relaxation takes place at its own pace. Benson practically paraphrases the anonymous fourteenth-century English monk who authored *The Cloud of Unknowing* in this statement, "When distracting thoughts occur, try to ignore them by not dwelling upon them and return to repeating 'One.'" The monk had said, "Should some thought go on annoying you, demanding to know what you are doing, answer with this one word alone."

Some six hundred years and a completely different conception of man and the universe separate the cloistered mystic from the modern medical researcher. But they are both giving exactly the same advice. Benson does not take offense at being called unoriginal. "We claim no innovation," he has written, "but simply a scientific validation of age-old wisdom. The technique is our current method of eliciting the Relaxation Response."

As word of Benson's work began to reach the general public, TMers reacted first more in sorrow than in anger. Benson, they said, was using the trappings of meditation, but had missed its essence. That could be attained only through following the exact

instructions laid down by the Maharishi—compulsory lectures, secret mantra, fresh flowers and all. Ironically a very similar charge had often been leveled against TM by practitioners of more rigorous spiritual disciplines. They had said that TM was too easy and just a gimmick.

Then Benson wrote up his theories in a book called *The Relaxation Response*. The book got an enormous amount of publicity, and rapidly rose to the top of the best-seller list. A few months earlier, an entirely orthodox book on TM by Harold H. Bloomfield, M.D. and several coauthors had been on the top of the best-seller list. This book, and several other popular TM books, had been written by meditators and had all insisted that one had to go through the TM program, and that TM could not be learned from a book. A number of other books had come out explaining exactly how TM worked, and suggesting methods of meditating by using a nonsecret mantra, or simply a word like "One." None of these earlier books had the impact of Benson's, though the advice was essentially the same.

Benson's name had been linked so closely with TM that it appeared as if he was a major defector from the cause—although he wasn't. To many it seemed the book revealed the "secrets" of TM, though there are no secrets except the mantra. It also seemed that all the benefits of a $125 TM course could be obtained through the purchase of a $5 book (later a $1.95 paperback). RR was not only cheaper than TM, it was simpler.

At about the time that Benson's book was rising in the best-seller charts, enrollments in TM programs, which had been growing consistently for several years, began to level off and then decline. Had Benson's do-it-yourself relaxation set back the Maharishi's World Plan? Of course there is no way of really knowing. The ups and downs of public interest in such a sub-

ject as TM are hard to explain and impossible to predict. But there could be little doubt that Herbert Benson's *The Relaxation Response* had hurt the cause of TM, at least temporarily. The public was now aware that there was an alternate and even simpler method of achieving some of the same results.

One reaction appeared in the November 3, 1975, issue of *Publishers Weekly*, the bible of the book publishing industry. It was a two-page ad, half of it a parody clearly aimed at Benson's *The Relaxation Response*. The headline read:

"Quit selling our customers books that claim open-heart surgery can only be performed by highly trained professionals!"

Below the headline was a reproduction of what was supposed to be the cover of a book called *Open-Heart Surgery Self-Taught*. The author was "Dr. Hugo Eckuno, D.D.S." The advertisement went on to read: "This book teaches anyone how to perform open-heart surgery on themselves in their own home using common kitchen instruments." Some of the chapters listed were: "Scalpel vs. Paring Knife: Is There Really Any Difference?" and "How to Turn a Transistor Radio into a Pacemaker."

The spoof was funny, the sort of humor that appears in college humor magazines and the *National Lampoon*. But it was also mean. Those who had put together the parody were angry.

The reason for the joke was made clear on the facing page. "Unfortunately," read this side of the ad, "not everything can be learned from a book. Open-heart surgery is one of them. The Transcendental Meditation technique is another." The ad then went on to criticize other methods of meditation as being inferior to TM, and wound up by recommending four orthodox books about the TM program.

Benson's book was not criticized directly, but that is only because *Publishers Weekly* had the authors of the ad tone down

their original version. In many fields it is common for manufacturers of one product to directly criticize their competitors, but *Publishers Weekly* apparently felt that such a direct assault on *The Relaxation Response* by the supporters of a rival technique was out of line. Even in the toned-down version the point was made.

Printed at the bottom of the ad was the statement that it had been paid for by twenty-eight persons who practice the TM program. The moving force behind the ad, however, was Peter McWilliams, coauthor of a popular and orthodox TM book. But McWilliams was not just out to protect the profits of his own popular book from encroachments of an even more popular rival. Like many other devoted TMers, he was genuinely outraged at Benson. The ad had begun as sort of a bitter joke circulated among like-minded meditators. There is no indication that the official TM leadership in any way authorized this attack upon Benson.

The reaction of the TM officials to Benson and *The Relaxation Response* has been more restrained and moderate. Jerry Jarvis, national director of the TM movement, insists that TM is entirely natural and spontaneous, and does not involve any degree of "concentration." Benson's method, and others like it, involve concentration on breathing or repeating a word, says Jarvis. While he concedes that such a technique might produce a form of relaxation, it would be a dulling relaxation. TM, he says, results in mental clarity. Besides, people would soon get bored with any method that involves concentration.

It is difficult to understand this particular criticism. Why does saying "One" involve any more concentration than saying a Sanskrit word? Benson does not ask his subjects to concentrate on their breathing as do Zen meditators; he merely uses

breathing as a convenient method of counting. In testing the Benson method myself, I found it quite easy to silently repeat "One" with every breath. There was no concentration or effort involved. The method can be learned in five minutes. You can try it yourself from the instructions given on the previous pages.

Boredom is another matter. The Benson method produced, in me at least, a tendency to doze off. Sleep may be relaxing but it does not produce the same physiological effects as meditating.

More significantly, people may become bored with the method and simply stop using it. No matter how effective any particular relaxation or meditation technique may be, it is of little use if people won't stick to it. Is there something about TM that will make people more willing to keep meditating? No one can say for sure, but the devotees of TM are certainly passionately attached to their practice. As already mentioned, even casual meditators have a fairly good record of continuing their meditation. Benson's method has not been around long enough to have acquired much of a record in this area.

Another point that Jarvis makes is that personal contact between novice meditator and teacher is important, for it helps to motivate the meditator. There is also TM's follow-up program of checking. None of this is available from a technique learned through a book.

Jarvis was dubious about the use of the word "One" or any other random word in place of a personally chosen Sanskrit mantra. The random word, he says, might contain the wrong vibrations for the individual who is using it. Simply picking a word is, in Jarvis' view, a bit like taking an untested medicine. TM, he insists, is a technique that has been tested by thousands of years of tradition. It involves no experimentation, and is entirely safe and fully effective.

But in the matter of the proper "vibrations" of the mantra and the effectiveness of ancient traditions, we slip over into an area which is beyond the reach of scientific investigation. Clearly such beliefs underlie the practice of TM, but they are not usually emphasized; rather, emphasis is placed on scientific validation. It is scientific validation, not ancient tradition, that has made TM so popular.

And that is another area of criticism that TMers have of the Benson technique. The effectiveness of TM claims, they say, has been validated in over three hundred scientific studies. Benson's relaxation response has had nowhere near that much testing. Most of the positive results that have been obtained for it have come from Benson's own research team.

Benson himself has maintained an extremely low profile in this controversy. He seems genuinely anxious not to get into a public fight with TM, which he considers to be an effective method of producing the relaxation response, but not the only method.

Benson's claims for his technique are comparatively modest. He says it can produce relaxation and help protect the body against many of today's stress-related illnesses, particularly high blood pressure. TM starts with such claims and goes on to insist that their method will increase personal happiness, fulfillment, and creativity, and ultimately will transform the world into a better place to live. Moreover, says TMers, these extended claims can be scientifically documented.

Let us examine some of these claims. In the first place, TM is quite correct in insisting that their method has been frequently tested, whereas the Benson method has not, and that there is not enough data for directly comparing the overall effectiveness of the two methods.

The statement that "further research is needed" is the great

scientific cop-out. Whenever confronting a difficult question a scientist may avoid taking a stand by insisting that "further research is needed." Further research is almost always needed, but in the relaxation controversy, further research really is needed. Benson's methods simply have not been around long enough to receive the sort of long-term testing that is necessary.

The testing is not going to be easy either. Attempting to compare the reactions of TMers and practitioners of the relaxation response would first involve trying to discover whether different sorts of people took up different methods. Just picking ten of one discipline and ten of the other, and measuring their blood pressure and brain waves, is not good enough.

TMers say that after meditating they feel more happy, fulfilled, energetic, "together," and creative than when they started. Such abstract concepts are difficult to test, and one must often rely on individual subjective evaluations. These are hardly scientific, but they are all we have, and they can be interesting.

C. Eugene Moore, M.D., a New York City physician, used the Benson method and the TM program. He described his reactions for writer Martin Ebon's book *The Relaxation Controversy*. Dr. Moore found both methods roughly comparable. He found that no noticeable personal changes took place as the result of either method. The quality of both experiences seemed about the same, though he liked the fact that the TM mantra was not linked to breathing. However, Dr. Moore said that he would recommend the Benson technique to his patients "because it is free."

Fee paying was not necessarily a bad thing, Dr. Moore noted. "Many people need some mild coercement in the form of paying $125 and following a certain rigid discipline in the introductory course as TM has to offer. The Benson technique is totally self-

policed, so to speak. The public relations aspect and teaching characteristics of the TM program are highly beneficial to a great many people, I believe, people who will not otherwise casually perform a technique which seems so simple as described by Benson."

Others have pointed out that the whole mystic aura which surrounds TM tends to give people a greater belief in it and higher expectations from it. The more one believes and the more one expects, the more one is likely to get. So the flowers and the secrecy and the lectures may all be extremely useful, though not for the reasons that TM devotees believe.

A negative side to this is that greater expectations may also produce greater disappointments. If all the helpful changes promised by TM do not take place, this can lead people to drop meditation entirely, even though it is doing them some good.

Newspaper columnist Phyllis Battelle had tried both methods and described her experiences in an article in *The Ladies' Home Journal*. She had been an enthusiast for TM, but when the Benson book came out she was urged by friends to try his method.

Mrs. Battelle did find a difference in the two methods. While TM meditation made her feel energetic, Benson's method, she said, made her "pleasantly drowsy." Occasionally TM gave her an experience beyond relaxation, "that delicious moment when the hands and feet suddenly seem to float, while the body is nonexistent." She did not get this from the Benson method. She also felt that TM was easier. "It [the Benson method] demands a certain mental thrust to establish a rate of breathing, a rate of thought. TM is simple but infinitely delicate."

In Phyllis Battelle's opinion, TM delivered an "extra dimension" not promised or delivered by the Relaxation Response.

This, of course, is an entirely subjective view, which may

have been influenced by the fact that Mrs. Battelle was already deeply committed to TM. "But I have been spoiled by TM meditation. I would rather transcend than switch."

Any meditation method can produce its subjective devotees. TM's primary claim to fame—and one that has frequently been used in TM's public relations battle with Benson's Relaxation Response and other relaxation and meditation methods—is that TM's claims have been validated in over three hundred scientific studies.

The most famous of these studies is the original 1970 Benson and Wallace study. It is still the study most frequently cited in TM literature. It must be noted, however, that not all scientists who have attempted to repeat the Benson and Wallace study have obtained such striking results. Though virtually every study shows that TM does promote relaxation, Benson's own studies indicate that his method appears to work as well. Studies of other admittedly more rigorous and difficult methods of meditation also indicate that they promote a very relaxed state.

In addition to promoting relaxation there are also a number of studies which show that people who take up TM tend to cut down on drug abuse, excessive drinking and smoking. There are also studies which show that TM improves on-the-job performance and reduces employee absenteeism. So impressive have these results been that TM has been sponsored by a wide variety of diverse organizations, from government drug abuse programs for their patients to large companies for their employees.

But the critics have not been silenced. Psychologist Robert E. Ornstein has gone so far as to accuse TM of "hucksterism" in its use of science to promote itself. In his book *The Mind Field*, Ornstein complains:

"In the case of TM, the bulk of its claimed scientific 'valida-

tions' are usually marked 'submitted for publication'—or are published by the movement's own Maharishi International University Press. Such claims constitute a debasement of both science and meditation. Here, science is employed to document improvements in personality, or bodily changes, with no consideration given to whether such changes are in fact due to meditation, and what the significance of the change really is."

One of the major claims made by TM is that the technique increases creativity. TM is sometimes called "The Science of Creative Intelligence." Now creativity is one of those qualities that is hard to define and even harder to measure. Any claim to scientific validation of increased creativity immediately puts the claimant on slippery ground. There are a variety of tests for creativity, though there is little agreement as to how good they are.

But even leaving aside all of those reservations, the results for TM and creativity have been ambiguous. Harvard psychologist Gary Schwartz gave a variety of creativity tests to a group of sixteen teachers of TM and a group of sixteen controls. On one type of test the teachers scored consistently better than the controls, but on other kinds of tests they did no better, or actually got lower scores. Schwartz concluded that too much meditation might actually interfere with creativity.

Schwartz theorizes that creativity actually involves two stages, an initial stage where the idea emerges, and a more active stage where the idea is expressed. While meditation might aid in the initial stage, it might hinder the expression of creative ideas.

This discussion merely scratches the surface of the controversy surrounding the scientific "validation" of TM's claims. The problem is an extremely complex one. Many people think that with a couple of experiments or studies scientists can

prove something true, or untrue. Unfortunately, it usually isn't that simple, particularly in areas involving human behavior.

But there is little disagreement that TM, and perhaps similar systems as well, do promote a helpful, healthful relaxation. This is not the main aim of TM or other forms of meditation, but it is not a small accomplishment. TM has also aided greatly in making meditation a respectable subject in the West. While many scientists will still disagree strongly about the overall value of TM, there is little doubt that the Maharishi's system is largely responsible for a whole new Western attitude toward meditation. A lot more people are willing to take the subject seriously. That is no small accomplishment either.

5

Meditation and the Brain

The current excitement and controversy over meditation and relaxation has almost obscured a fundamental fact about the practice. Thousands of years of tradition and effort in meditation have not been aimed at helping people relax and lower their blood pressure. Using meditation as a relaxing technique is a relatively new development, and one that yogis, sufis, and the rest would consider a trivial one.

Many teachers of meditation may say that it is impossible without physical relaxation. Eastern philosophies and religions tend to make no sharp distinction between body and mind. Yet certain active meditation techniques—for example, dervish dancing—are certainly not relaxing in the ordinary sense of the word. Meditation is primarily a mental process. The major and most important changes that take place during meditation should take place in the brain. That is very unfortunate for those of us who wish to explain meditation, for the brain is very largely unexplored territory.

Western science is reasonably good at measuring bodily relaxation, but scientific measurements of mental activity are still at a very primitive stage. However, the newcomer to meditation who encounters some highly publicized meditation techniques might not know just how primitive the scientific measurement of mental activity is. He is apt to become confused and unduly impressed by talk of brain waves and the glory of "the alpha state."

A little background is necessary here. The brain, like other parts of a living organism, generates a small but measurable amount of electricity. Through the use of a machine called an electroencephalograph this electrical activity can be picked up, amplified, and displayed in a visual form by a pen tracing a jagged line across a piece of moving graph paper. It is this visual representation of the electrical activity within the brain that we call "brain waves."

In order for an electroencephalogram or EEG to be taken, electrodes must be pasted or otherwise attached to the subject's scalp. A good electroencephalograph is an expensive and cumbersome piece of equipment. Its use requires a trained operator. Proper interpretation of the brain wave record also requires professional expertize.

Scientists have identified four basic brain wave types, or states. They are called alpha, beta, delta, and theta, after the letters in the Greek alphabet. The fastest of these waves are the beta, a pattern generally associated with an awake and alert state. The alpha pattern is the one that has always attracted the most attention. It is the easiest to identify and is generally associated with a relaxed but awake state. Delta and theta waves have appeared most frequently in sleeping subjects.

The alpha waves were the first to be identified when the EEG

was developed back in the 1920s. That is why these waves were given the first letter of the Greek alphabet. Most early EEG tests were given to subjects who were sitting or lying down with their eyes closed. It is when a person is relaxing in this way that alpha waves appear most frequently.

For years it was believed that brain waves were entirely beyond conscious control. Then in the 1950s Joe Kamiya, who was doing research in sleep at the University of Chicago, almost accidentally stumbled across the discovery that people could consciously put themselves into the alpha state. The finding that conscious control of the brain waves is possible was revolutionary in the field of brain physiology.

Kamiya and others began training people to increase their production of alpha waves through a process called biofeedback. The theory of biofeedback holds that if a person knows what is going on with such internal functions as brain waves, he can, to a considerable degree, control that function.

Electroencephalographs were set up so that when alpha brain waves appeared a low hum or some other particular sound or tone could be heard. The subjects tried to keep the tone going, and they could. A lot of people found this enormously exciting. Soon there was a virtual alpha feedback cult of people who kept trying to "turn on" their alpha.

When researchers began taking brain wave readings from meditators it was discovered that they were exceptionally good at attaining and holding the alpha state for long periods, far longer than untrained individuals.

Most people reported that they found the alpha state pleasurable and relaxing. A small number reported exhilarating, even transcendental, feelings in alpha, while a smaller number still found the experience depressing or frightening. As all of this

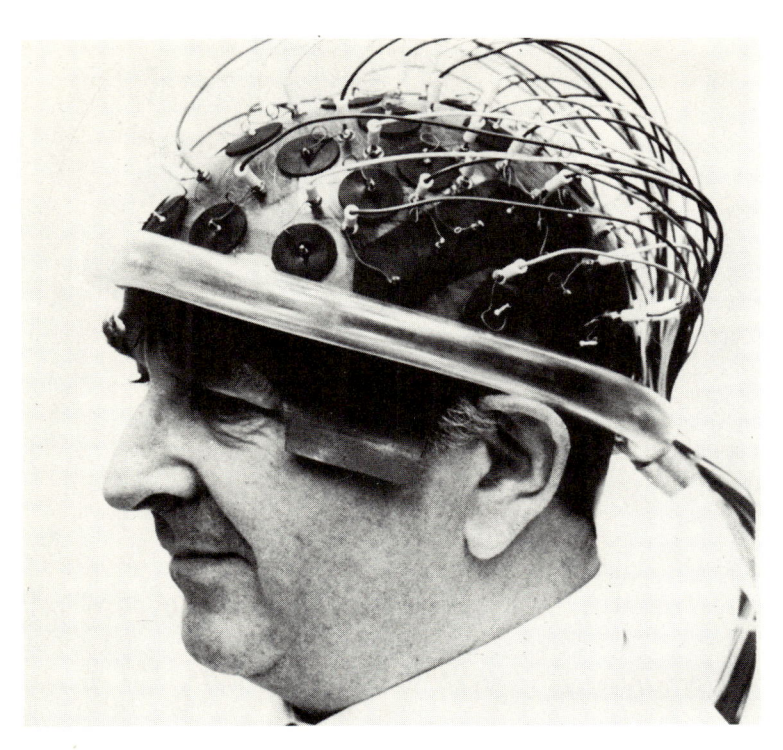

Brain waves are measured by electrodes attached to the scalp.

information about alpha brain waves began to tumble out of the laboratories it was picked up by the general public, but often in a garbled and incomplete way. The result was that a lot of people got the idea that there was something terribly special about alpha. It was said that the "alpha state" was some sort of instant Zen or instant yoga. A few biofeedback enthusiasts suggested that through the use of their system a person could get the equivalent of years of meditation training in months or even days. None of these enthusiastic predictions has been fulfilled, and today the bloom is off the alpha biofeedback craze.

There isn't necessarily anything special about producing alpha waves. If you wish to experience the "alpha state" all

that you have to do is make yourself comfortable, relax, and close your eyes. If you were hooked to an electroencephalograph it would probably begin registering alpha waves. The feeling can be pleasant enough, but it does not automatically bring one to a state of "enlightenment" or anything else. Some scientists now believe that alpha is produced when the brain is idling.

More recent research has indicated that some experienced meditators go from alpha to theta and even to delta while in deep meditation. The meditators are distinctly awake, and delta and theta waves are rare in waking subjects who are not meditators. Kamiya has suggested that meditation may produce a highly individualized pattern of brain waves in different people. There is no single universal brain wave pattern for meditation.

A major problem in relating meditation, or any other mental process, to brain waves is that the EEG record provides only the grossest sort of measurement of brain activity. Psychologist Robert Ornstein, who has worked extensively with EEGs, is extremely careful about drawing any major conclusions from these measurements alone.

"...the mere report of an alteration in the electroencephalogram," he has written, "means almost nothing by itself. The EEG alone is quite an unstable measure, and rigorous controls must be maintained to ensure that it actually relates to significant brain activity. Recording an EEG might be compared to placing a heat sensor over a computer and attempting thereby to determine the computer's program."

In medicine the EEG is used primarily to aid in the diagnosis of such severe illnesses as epilepsy, or major brain damage. Most recently the EEG has been used as the final determination of whether a person is alive or dead. Today, stopped hearts

can be restarted. The heart and lungs can be kept working by artificial means. But once electrical activity within the brain ceases, doctors agree that death is irreversible. There is no way known, or even reasonably imagined, of restarting a stopped brain.

So the EEG can tell us when a person's brain is damaged, or when a person is dead. But meditators and non-meditators alike produce alpha waves. There is no known difference in brain wave patterns between a happy and fulfilled person, and a miserable and frustrated one. There is no brain wave pattern which separates the genius from the mediocre mind.

TM practitioners were among those shown to be exceptionally good at producing alpha. Yet despite the fact that TM has been quick to seize upon anything that looked like scientific validation for its practice, the movement largely avoided the excesses of the alpha cult. TM was downright hostile toward alpha biofeedback, claiming that it could not produce "true meditation" and was unnecessary, to boot. It was easier and cheaper to boost alpha production through a TM course than through alpha biofeedback training, they said. Experiments have backed up this statement.

Still, TM has made some exaggerated claims in regard to brain waves. One of the more interesting ones is that during TM the two hemispheres of the brain work in harmony because the brain waves from each of the hemispheres show "increased synchrony," that is, they are more alike.

Now the fact that our brains have two separate and distinct halves, or hemispheres, that have different functions, and often seem to be working at cross-purposes with one another, is extremely significant. This may throw some light on what happens during meditation, and we will return to it in detail later. But

the TM claim of "increased synchrony" between brain hemispheres has been sharply questioned on two fronts.

First, the findings that TM publicizes have not been widely repeated in other studies. Repeatability is necessary in laboratory science, and it is absolutely essential in brain wave studies where so many minor and seemingly unimportant variables can change the results in a single study.

Secondly, does the fact that both hemispheres of the brain are generating the same types of brain waves really mean that they are working in harmony? Is this "increased synchrony," presuming it exists at all, of any importance? Is it good for you or bad for you? In fact, no one can say for sure. Nor does anyone know whether this "synchrony" is due to TM or might be produced by other practices.

All of this brings us back to the point that we really don't know a great deal about how the human brain operates. Instruments like the EEG help a little, but the major mysteries remain. To try and draw any major conclusions from a particular brain wave pattern, no matter how "smooth" and "restful" it may look when displayed on graph paper, is misleading.

Still, the EEG has been used to turn up some interesting observations about meditators. These indicate that the brain of a highly trained meditator does not operate exactly like that of an untrained individual.

In the early 1960s, Marion A. Wagner of UCLA and Basu K. Bagchi of the University of Michigan did some pioneering studies on Indian yogis. These tests showed that the yogis possessed superb control over their bodies. The control extended to such internal activities as heartbeat and blood pressure, which Western medical scientists had assumed to be entirely beyond conscious control. In terms of conventional medical and physio-

logical theory, the yogis were able to accomplish the impossible.

It is hardly surprising, therefore, that these yogis also showed a remarkable degree of control over the actions of their brains. While meditating, the EEGs of the yogis displayed strong alpha rhythms, often continuing for hours. You and I would soon find our minds wandering, or following a particular train of thought, and our EEGs would begin to show the faster beta waves of ordinary waking consciousness. Noise or other distractions would disrupt the alpha waves, and ultimately we might fall asleep, which would produce yet another change in the EEG. None of this happened to the yogis.

Whatever else meditation might do for the yogis, it allowed them to reach and hold a particular brain wave state far longer than persons who had not received such training. A series of follow-up studies on meditating yogis conducted at the All-India Institute of Medical Science revealed just how deeply absorbed these meditators were in their work. Imagine that you are sitting quietly, relaxing with your eyes closed, yet still fully awake. Your brain is at that moment most likely registering alpha waves. Then there is a soft noise nearby. You probably won't jump, or show any external reaction. An outside observer could not tell whether you heard the noise or not. But the noise will break your alpha pattern, at least briefly. Psychologists call this the "startle reaction." It is entirely involuntary, and scientists believed that everyone had such a reaction, whether they were aware of it or not.

Yogis had always insisted that while meditating they could remain fully awake, yet entirely shut out the external world. Western scientists had doubted the claim, for they assumed that the yogis, like everyone else, had a startle reaction. The yogis just looked impassive and unmoved, and perhaps they were not

even aware of the reaction, but it would show up on the EEG. The Indian tests revealed that a soft but audible sound did not break the alpha pattern of the meditating yogis. The very same yogis just sitting quietly, but not meditating, showed the standard startle reaction when tested with the same sound. The yogis had not been exaggerating their powers. While meditating and sitting quietly look the same, they are not.

Japanese researchers Akira Kasamatsu and Tomio Hirai tested forty masters of zazen. There are some important differences between zazen and yoga meditation. An obvious one is that the Zen meditators have their eyes open during meditation, while the yoga meditators keep their eyes closed. Zen meditators say that they are aware of what is going on around them, but are entirely detached from it.

The Zen meditators began producing steady alpha patterns after only a minute or two of sitting with their eyes open. This was unusual in itself, for it had been thought that alpha could be produced only with the eyes closed. The alpha pattern grew stronger and slower as the meditation continued. In the more experienced of the meditators, the even slower theta waves began to appear after about half an hour.

The startle reaction of the Zen meditators was then tested. During the meditation period a series of twenty soft clicks, repeated at regular fifteen-second intervals, was produced. The EEGs showed that the meditators had reacted with a momentary disruption in their alpha rhythm. After a few seconds the alpha rhythm was reestablished as if nothing had happened. The same reaction was recorded to all of the clicks in the series.

The yogis, you will recall, showed no reaction in a similar test. Control subjects who were just sitting there with their eyes closed had yet a third reaction. The first click completely

Zen meditators are aware of what is going on around them, but are not distracted by it.

blocked the alpha waves as the controls exhibited a strong reaction. But the control subjects quickly got used to the noise. By the fourth click in the series the startle reaction had disappeared. The Zen meditators did not show a strong startle reaction, but they never got used to the clicks either. They continued to show the same mild reaction throughout the entire series.

Yogis had always insisted that they were able to block out all outside stimuli during meditation. They startled scientists by blocking out the startle reaction. The Zen meditators were also able to do what they said they could, though few Western scientists had thought it possible.

Neither yogis nor practitioners of zazen meditate in order to control their brain waves. For centuries meditators were not even aware that there were such things as brain waves, and the majority probably still don't know, and if they do know, don't care.

Scientists are still not sure what the brain waves signify in any detail. But one thing that these tests did indicate was that highly trained meditators were far more aware of their states of consciousness than most of us would be. We rarely spend time or effort thinking about our mental state. It has been pointed out that the Hindus have some twenty different names for varying states of consciousness, while in English there are only a few names.

Brain wave researcher Joe Kamiya publicly deplores the fact that "we have not been trained to name various psychological states." He hopes that someday the West will have developed a more precise "vocabulary of moods."

Meditation does other things to the brain in addition to altering brain wave patterns. Robert Ornstein has pointed out that continual concentration, be it on an object or a word, produces some definite biological effects upon the brain. All forms of meditation, whether they are of the mantra-type, audible chanting, dancing, or whatever, involve continual concentration. Zen meditation, with its insistence upon "attention," very obviously involves continual concentration.

TM, on the other hand, insists that it is "entirely natural" and that no concentration is required. However, the continual repetition of a Sanskrit mantra is quite obviously what Ornstein and other psychologists would class as a form of continual concentration, no matter what TM devotees wish to call it.

The biological effects upon the brain produce certain feelings, moods, or experiences which can be interpreted differently. The interpretation often depends upon what a person expects. If one expects to receive some truly transcendental experience, he may feel he has received one.

Ornstein says that when a person concentrates on a single

stimulus, like a mantra, long enough the stimulus itself seems eventually to disappear, leaving pure attention without content. The feeling is a novel one, and the person deeply involved in TM or some other form of meditation might consider such a feeling highly significant. The Maharishi has often spoken of meditators reaching a state of "pure consciousness."

There are many other novel mental experiences that continual concentration may produce. These range from a feeling of loss of contact with external reality to seeing white lights and even visions of the deity. But how significant are such experiences? To the novice meditator they can appear extremely significant, even overwhelming. They are "peak experiences" and sometimes one feels that he or she has reached "enlightenment" or achieved a state of "expanded consciousness." But most psychologists who are interested in meditation, as well as many highly trained meditators, will agree that such experiences, while they can be striking, are not necessarily of great significance.

Practitioners of Zen are particularly unimpressed by such dramatic events. Many of these fall under the heading of what they call *Makyo*, a form of illusion. Makyo is considered a necessary part of training in meditation, but not the goal. One is reminded of the story of the Zen master whose student had seen a bright light with the Buddha behind it. "Concentrate on your breathing," the student was told, "and it will go away."

The *Suringama Sutra*, an ancient Indian set of instructions in mysticism, lists fifty different types of illusions that may interrupt the meditator in his work, and then goes on to say that such illusions are only the most common types.

St. Gregory of Sinai, in his instructions on meditation, observed, "When, while you work you see within or without you a light or a flame or an image—of Christ, for example, or of an

angel, or of someone else—do not accept it lest you suffer harm. And do not yourself create fantasies nor pay attention to those that create themselves."

Repeating a word or short phrase over and over again can make it sound rather odd, so odd in fact that the effect can be very dramatic. British psychologist Christopher Evans, in writing about Hare Krishna chanting, noted:

"In fact psychologists know that when a word or brief phrase is repeated over and over again, it begins to change its characteristics in a peculiar way. This is not merely a matter of tongue-twisting (Hare Krishna soon becomes pretty muddled on repetition) for a word played repeatedly on a tape recorder will soon distort perceptually in the most strange way. The word kettle, for example, will soon be heard as petal, castle, rattle, etc. The phenomenon, which is an exceedingly striking one and which anyone can demonstrate to himself with a tape recorder and an endless loop of tape, has been the subject of much serious psychological experimentation and is believed to say something about the nature of the auditory recognition process. It is very likely that this odd effect is behind the evolution of the mantra, a phrase or prayer which repeated over and over again is supposed to acquire a special kind of spiritual significance. . ."

Could the ancient and revered practice of mantra meditation be based on a quirk of our hearing? Christopher Evans seems to think so.

Well, if it is not visions, or "peak experiences," that are the primary aim of meditation, what is? We will return to that most difficult and intriguing question in a later chapter. But first we have to deal with some problems, for the practice of meditation is not without its diversions and even its dangers.

6

Fears and Fantasies

Just a few years ago there were very few in the United States who practiced meditation. It wasn't controversial then. Now millions meditate. The explosive growth of this ancient practice may represent a significant social change in America. Now meditation is often controversial.

While some people welcome this sort of social change, many others resist it. The importation or, to be more accurate, the reintroduction of meditation from the Orient has worried, angered, and frightened a lot of people. They look upon it as alien, potentially destructive, faintly sinister, even diabolical. These fears have generated some open hostility toward the practice. While meditation, in general, has enjoyed a friendly reception in the U.S., as its popularity grows so does the opposition.

Many of the fears of meditation are utterly unfounded, based on misinformation, lack of information, or simple prejudice. Others have some substance. But whatever their origin, the fears

are deeply felt. We are going to try to deal with some of them in this chapter.

One often hears that meditation is some strange, exotic, Oriental activity. In fact, most of the meditation being practiced today has come from the East, but as we have already seen, meditation is not unknown in either Judaism or Christianity. It has just fallen into disuse in modern times. If one considers that some of the American nature mystics of the nineteenth century, like Henry David Thoreau, also meditated in their own way, one might conclude that meditation is as American as apple pie. Still, you must admit that the currently popular forms of meditation originated in India, and to a lesser extent Japan and other Eastern countries.

In the minds of many people meditation is also linked with psychoactive or psychedelic drugs like LSD. Yet virtually all meditators, no matter what particular technique they use or what school they follow, deplore drugs. TM boasts that after taking up their method most drug users stop. Strict sects like the Hare Krishnas have an absolute ban on all stimulants.

Yet the confusion of meditation and drugs is in some ways inevitable. It is even fair to say that the current interest in meditation really began with psychoactive drugs back in the early 1960s. Among the promises made for such drugs was that they would expand consciousness, and make life more fulfilling and creative. Some drug enthusiasts even thought that the drugs could bring an individual closer to God or Ultimate Reality, that they could produce a profound religious experience. But it never worked out that way.

A lot of people who had become disillusioned with the solutions that drugs offered were still very interested in finding answers to the questions that had led them to drugs in the first

place. The conventional answers were still unsatisfying. Many of these people then turned to meditation. I have seen no surveys on the subject, but it is reasonable to assume that a large percentage of those who got into meditation, particularly in the days when the practice was just becoming known in the U.S., had first been involved with drugs. Some meditation groups advertised themselves as a way to "turn on without drugs."

Take the case of Richard Alpert. Alpert, wealthy son of a railroad president, was a professor of psychology at Harvard during the early '60s. Along with another Harvard psychology professor, Timothy Leary, Alpert began experimenting with LSD, and soon moved from experimenter to evangelist for psychoactive drugs. Leary went on to become the high priest of the American drug culture, and public enemy number one in the eyes of many who hated and feared drugs. He also wound up in jail, from which he has only recently been paroled.

Alpert took another road. In 1967 he went to India where he met a Maharishi, not *the* Maharishi Mahesh Yogi of TM, but Neem Karoli Baba who is also known by the title Maharishi. Richard Alpert came back to the U. S. as Baba Ram Dass, and began teaching Indian philosophy to the same sort of enthusiastic college audiences that in an earlier time would have been attracted to lectures on drugs.

But there are no drugs in Ram Dass' philosophy now, nor are there in any of the other popular meditative teachings. Yet the aura of the drug culture persists, and makes meditation suspect to many.

Some Christian clergymen have accused meditation of being downright diabolical. This charge is leveled most sharply against TM, which tries so hard to be noncontroversial and not offend anyone's religious sensibilities.

To many Westerners the gods of Hinduism appear strange and diabolical-looking.

Part of the problem lies in the Hindu origins of TM. To some, Hinduism is an alien and idolatrous religion. People seem to pray to statues of strange-looking gods who often look more like devils. To call the ancient Hindu religion and all the practices which spring from it diabolical is merely the result of ignorance and intolerance.

Of course the ultimate aim of TM is not to bring the meditator to Jesus or to any other conventional Western religious concept. Therefore, it has been roundly condemned. But just because a practice is not Christian does not automatically make it diabolical. Still, there is more substance to the charge that meditation can be diabolical than simply a fear of strange gods.

Some ministers believe that during meditation the mind is emptied of godly thoughts and rendered receptive to diabolical ones. The fear sounds absolutely medieval if not primitive, but it isn't. If restated in different words it makes some sense.

One of the things that all forms of meditation are supposed to do is to eventually bring about an alteration of consciousness, to break down conventional and stereotyped ways of perceiving the world. One of the most common experiences reported by novice meditators is that they have begun to look at the world in a new way.

This is certainly one of the aims of TM, though the movement does not advertise the fact in quite that way. The official TM line is that TM will not change your day-to-day life, merely make it better and better. But one need not go too deeply into the writings and philosophy of the Maharishi to discover that fundamental changes in perception of the world is just exactly what he is after with his technique. TM provides no assurance that the meditator will be a better churchgoer. There are many who do not wish to see traditional ways of perceiving shattered, who

think that it is downright dangerous. When this happens, they feel, the young and impressionable can be left defenseless against strange influences which might indeed be diabolical.

As a practical matter there is little danger that the casual meditator who does his or her two brief sessions each day in order to relax, or simply because it is fashionable, is going to undergo any great personality changes. Even the severest critics of TM are hard put to come up with any examples of people who have become "possessed" or otherwise deranged by taking up TM. Yet the fear is always there.

Deep involvement with a movement like TM is irreconcilable with most conservative religions. Strict sects like the Hare Krishnas are obviously incompatible with all other religions. They make no bones about it. You can't be a Hare Krishna and attend church at the same time.

The spectre of "brainwashing" is often raised in connection with meditation. Today brainwashing is a popular word, and a scary one. It's used so often that one might get the impression that it has a precise scientific meaning, but it doesn't. There is even a good deal of controversy over whether there is such a thing as brainwashing at all.

The term "brainwashing" first entered the English language during the Korean War. Many American prisoners of war were subjected to extremely harsh conditions. They were not exactly tortured, though they were occasionally beaten, kept in isolation, humiliated, and given an insufficient and monotonous diet. At the same time they were assailed by an almost constant propaganda barrage aimed at making them confess to war crimes that they never committed, and declare that they had been on the wrong side during the war. A lot of POWs signed confessions or made public statements simply to ease their plight, and

MEDITATION: WHAT IT CAN DO FOR YOU

who can blame them? But a small percentage actually underwent change and temporarily believed what they were saying. A few even elected to stay with their captors after the war was over and they had a chance to go home.

The Korean POW experience was a profound shock to the American people. American soldiers were not supposed to do that sort of thing. The impression got around that the "sinister Orientals" had developed some new and mysterious techniques which could turn good American boys into mindless robots. This impression was fed by a host of books and movies that presented "brainwashing" as some kind of magical mind control.

The U.S. military conducted an intensive investigation of Korean POWs after the war. One of the primary conclusions of this investigation was that many prisoners had succumbed to Korean pressures because they had been poorly trained, did not know what to expect, and were poorly motivated. The Korean War had never been popular and many soldiers did not think they should have been fighting there in the first place.

The war in Vietnam was even more unpopular than the Korean war had been. American POWs were often subjected to the same sort of brutal prison camp treatment, yet their reactions were very different. Why was the Vietnam experience different? Most of the American POWs in Vietnam were pilots shot down over North Korea. They were well-trained, highly motivated professionals who were well prepared for what they might have to face while imprisoned.

There is a vast amount of information about the experience of prisoners, or inmates in concentration camps, which strongly indicates that the North Koreans and the North Vietnamese had no mysterious all-powerful techniques for altering people's minds. There is an old saying that "everybody has a breaking

point." The Inquisition knew that centuries ago, and even St. Joan confessed to being a heretic, though she later recanted.

Yet the aura of the mysterious and the irresistible has clung to the term "brainwashing." A century ago the same sort of atmosphere surrounded the word "hypnosis." Unorthodox religious groups were often accused of "hypnotizing" their converts. Before that, converts were "bewitched." Today they are "brainwashed." It all comes to much the same thing.

The charge is utterly absurd when applied to a simple technique like TM. There is nothing of the prison camp about sitting quietly repeating a mantra.

But we can't just leave the problem there. Let's drop the supercharged word "brainwashing," and state the accusation another way. Can meditation be used as a method of controlling a person's thoughts and actions in any way? There is absolutely no evidence that brief regular meditation can. But prolonged meditation, particularly by an inexperienced person, might possibly be used as a method of thought control.

Journalist Ken Kelly, who had investigated the Guru Maharaj Ji's Divine Light Mission, saw meditation, as practiced within that group at least, as a sinister force. Many serious questions had been raised about the Guru and his methods and aims. Two of the Guru's close associates had been accused of beating and nearly killing a young man who had hit the Guru with a pie. So Kelly wrote in *The New York Times*:

"When the mind cannot answer any of the questions on the road to *satori*, it is the mind that must be annihilated, not the road that must be re-examined...

"Guru Maharaj Ji instills in his followers a mind control device that would surely make the Central Intelligence Agency envious. Called 'The Knowledge,' it is a combination of several

ancient yoga meditation techniques that members must practice several times a day, and particularly when the mind threatens to reassert its rational thrust. So when the Guru's ostensible message of peace and love is overshadowed by the violent practice that can accompany it, a follower can purge the mind of all contradictions by meditating them into oblivion."

Comparison of meditation with "mind control device" is a bit extreme. However, the thrust of Kelly's comments must be considered carefully, and not only in relation to the type of meditation practiced by those who followed the Divine Light Mission. Meditation is a means of quieting the mind, and blocking out troublesome questions. Remember that the English mystic who wrote *The Cloud of Unknowing* stated, "Should some thought go on annoying you, demanding to know what you are doing, answer with this one word alone." Instead of confronting a dilemma or problem, one simply meditates, and feels better, but the dilemma or problem remains. Meditation can be used as a way of avoiding distressing realities.

While it is not inevitable that meditation be used as a method of covering over troubling questions about gurus and other leaders of meditation movements, the possibility certainly exists. This possibility is especially worrisome because the movements which practice meditation, at least the large and well-known ones, have a strong tendency toward autocratic leaders, often with divine pretensions. Guru-worship is epidemic in modern meditation.

The Guru Maharaj Ji very nearly said he was God. Prabhupada, leader of the Hare Krishnas, doesn't say he is divine, but doesn't deny it either. Gurdjieff and Oskar Ichazo were somewhere between a father figure and an absolute dictator of their movements. One can hardly speak to a devoted TMer without

FEARS AND FANTASIES

being struck forcefully by the fact that the Maharishi is, to him, much more than just a respected teacher. His words are not guidelines, they are Holy Writ.

Once again we must emphasize the difference between brief regular periods of meditation, and full-time devotion to a severe meditation-oriented sect like the Hare Krishnas. The average TMer who goes no further with the practice than his twice daily meditations is in little danger of being controlled into doing anything. The Hare Krishna devotee, who must spend hours a day in chanting and devotions, may have little time for seriously entertaining searching questions about the path he has chosen. Questioning is certainly not encouraged.

Meditation is a nonrational practice, that is, during meditation the mind is not employed in dealing with problems in a logical step-by-step fashion. In the West it is generally taught that rational, logical thought is the only acceptable way of using one's mind. Most meditative disciplines deny this, and some go considerably farther. They regard the rational mind as "the enemy" and the seat of all human problems. Only through the nonrational act of meditation can one come to a true understanding of Reality. The rational mind must not only be ignored, it must be actively suppressed.

Typically, it was the Guru Maharaj Ji who stated this position most baldly and aggressively:

"Do you know, the devil is the son of man that comes to mind, through mind, from mind." Questioning, he said, "creates terrible suffering in your mind. You cannot sleep at night because of the illusive question."

Statements like the one just quoted are eagerly seized upon by those who fear and dislike all meditation. They are trotted out as proof that meditation is indeed a form of mind control, or

brainwashing. But many of those who are extremely friendly toward meditation also warn of the dangers of the extreme antirationalism that exists in many meditation groups.

Lawrence LeShan, a psychiatrist who has written extensively and sympathetically about meditation, has also said:

"Unfortunately, many in the group interested in meditation have fallen into one version of this trap and become remarkably anti-intellectual. Ideas, knowledge, intelligence are downgraded and disregarded in favor of experiences and of emotional and bodily expression. They say, in effect, 'We will only become whole by discarding part of ourselves and our heritage. Down with the cortex.' Their rebellion against being overcerebralized has led them to the opposite extreme, leading to a fragmentation equal to the one they were escaping."

Haridas Chaudhuri, professor of philosophy and president of the California Institute of Asian Studies, sees many pitfalls in systems like mantra meditation. He admits that such a technique may produce a peace of mind, even a temporary feeling of transcendental bliss, but for such feelings a heavy price must often be paid.

"It involves the suppression of one's independent thinking, resulting in incapacitation for critical evaluation of the value system handed by the guru. No thought structure or value system can possibly express the absolute truth. . . Unthinking identification with a particular value system may produce a wonderful sense of bliss, and that is perhaps all some people are capable of attaining—at least in this life. But such an identification also closes one's mind to the vastness of the real and confines it within a conceptual prison house. It produces, no doubt, some amount of liberation from worries and anxieties, but it also provides an escape from authentic freedom. . . .Pro-

viding an escape route from one kind of thought system from which the meditator felt alientated, it binds him hand and foot in another...."

Chaudhuri also warns of what he calls a "guru fixation." Typically, teachers of meditation present their systems as being the one and only true and absolutely valid one. Even when gurus do not proclaim their own divinity, disciples often consider them divine, and take all his utterances as supreme truth.

"If the guru is mature, he would of course take it upon himself to liberate the disciple in due time from his hypnotic spell. But an immature guru would naturally be inclined to perpetuate the situation for his personal glory or ego satisfaction."

Adulation and worship are powerful drugs. A leader with the best, and most humble, of intentions might begin to consider himself superhuman if all those around him kept telling him he was. So guru worship, or guru fixation, is a problem for leaders as well as followers.

Robert Ornstein questions the whole idea of guru glorification. Why, he wonders, must we bow down and bring flowers to a spiritual leader or teacher? He parallels the services of the guru to that of a surgeon.

"What sort of a surgeon would demand such behavior? He would not ask that a patient prostrate himself in order to obtain his specialized service, even though he may be the only one specially trained to aid in a life-threatening situation. One does not forever owe one's life to a surgeon after an operation, though it may indeed have saved one's life or given him vision. We would consider such behavior obviously inappropriate submission, yet one who knew little of medicine might not."

There is also some evidence which indicates that prolonged periods of meditation can be dangerous, particularly for the

novice. Most meditation practiced in the West involves a form of mild sensory deprivation—that is, cutting one's self off from the usual sights and sounds of everyday living. A variety of studies have shown that sensory deprivation can create great mental anguish, and even an emotional breakdown in individuals who have underlying psychological and emotional problems.

While there is no clear and convincing medical evidence that prolonged meditation will cause a breakdown or other serious consequences even in susceptible individuals, there are many stories of such things happening. Practically all teachers of meditation insist that it must be approached slowly. The novice at zazen does not immediately go on a sesshin, which may involve upwards of ten hours a day of just sitting. If that is what one wishes, it is a goal which must be trained for, like an athlete.

No one can reasonably expect to learn the rules of tennis one day and go out and play a championship game a week later. But meditation looks simple, and we come from a culture in which the practice is not widely understood. The temptation to try and take on more than we can handle is great.

While meditation brings quiet of mind to most, in a small percentage of people it appears to do nothing but release anxieties, and make them feel worse. For such individuals a period of sitting silently lowers the barriers which usually keep anxiety in check. TM checkers report that some who begin the program report severe symptoms as a result of their first few meditative sessions.

Many popular meditation programs carry with them the promise, stated or implied, that they can solve all, or practically all, of your problems. Such a promise presents two dangers.

First, meditation may be used in place of more appropriate and effective solutions. Second, if meditation fails to deliver, the person might be tempted to abandon the practice entirely, instead of recognizing it as a useful, though limited, technique.

Another commonly expressed fear is that meditation will somehow or other make us passive and submissive. The most extreme expression of this fear is that meditation is part of a communist plot aimed at undermining the will of the American people. There are those who see everything they dislike as part of some sort of plot.

The basis for much of this fear is ignorance and prejudice. It comes from the stereotype of the "active" Westerner as opposed to the "passive and submissive" Oriental. But if recent history has taught us nothing else it should have taught us that the Oriental is far from "passive and submissive." We have repeatedly pointed out that meditation is not exclusively an Oriental practice, that it was once considered among the highest activities a Christian could undertake.

TM emphasizes that people who practice their type of meditation become more active and involved in the world, not less.

TM enthusiasts love to present testimonials from people who claim to have done better in their outside activities as a result of TM. These, which appeared in the best-seller *TM, Discovering Inner Energy and Overcoming Stress*, are quite typical.

The first comes from a college student:

"Since I began meditating, my whole perspective on school has changed. I was thinking of dropping out, but now I am beginning to see the purpose of being here in terms of my own growth toward fulfillment. The relationships of material in this course have made me think seriously of switching into pre-med."

Another came from a business executive:

"Soon after I began meditating I noticed a clarity of mind that was, obviously, an asset in business situations where the responsibility of decision requires the careful weighing of many factors. Also of the utmost importance was the development of a reliable confidence in myself. In times of intensified emotional stress previous to meditation, I would often become stubborn and inflexible. This inflexibility was an asset in that it was one of the factors that allowed me to stand under criticism, and helped carry me along the paths that I thought to be the best, but it stemmed from a lesser state of personal development. I now have the same or more determination but the roots are grounded in satisfaction and inner freedom. The feeling of reacting against has left, and in its place stands a firmness, growing inner peace and harmony."

Obviously TM is very interested in keeping its followers active and in the world.

Yet the images of the passive and inward-looking Oriental, and the active, outward-looking Westerner remain, and there is something in addition to ignorance and prejudice behind it. Even scientists like Joe Kamiya, who are sympathetic to meditation, see it in terms of differing East-West attitudes. Kamiya has written:

"Western man has tended to focus on the external world, assuming the internal world to be beyond control, except for what happens to it as a result of efforts toward goal achievement in the external world. Eastern man, on the other hand, appears to have focused more attention on achievements (knowledge and control) in his internal world, assuming the external world to be largely beyond control."

During those periods of Western history when meditation was most widely practiced, notably the Middle Ages, Western

man also assumed the external world to be largely beyond his control. With the growth of rationalism and science in the West, meditative practices declined. They came to be scorned as relics of superstition.

The work ethic which developed in the West held that every waking moment should either be spent working, or in some sort of "improving" activity, like reading. The work ethic has declined in the twentieth century, but the passion for constant activity has remained. Even our leisure time tends to be frantic. Witness the popularity of vacation tours which cover a dozen countries in as many days, or resorts where every waking moment is spent in some sort of planned activity.

One prerequisite of meditation is a quiet environment. Yet noise is the almost constant companion of those of us who live in the West, particularly in urban environments. Much noise is unavoidable, but a good deal of it is self-inflicted. When things get too quiet we turn on the television set, or the radio or phonograph. If there isn't some sort of noise in the air a lot of people get nervous. Many city people become downright panicky when they first venture into a quiet environment. I know several people who are unable to sleep while they are in the country, because they can't stand the silence.

It is just this sort of addiction to constant activity, and constant noise, that many physicians feel can be stress-producing, and harmful in the long run. Meditation, by providing a period of quiet, and inactivity, can help to break the addiction.

Herbert Benson identified "adoption of a passive attitude" as the single most important feature of meditative disciplines. Yet in a society where "winning" is widely regarded as the highest virtue, adopting a passive attitude, even for a brief period, seems wrong, even sinful. The only way that some

people can accept meditation at all is by reminding themselves that it is good for their health, and therefore an "improving" activity.

Some devotees of meditation not only say that modern Western life is too hurried, too noisy, and too goal-oriented, they say that it is entirely worthless. They join the Hare Krishnas or some equally severe sect, and attempt to withdraw themselves from the mainstream of modern American life. Often they will claim that true meditation is not possible without adopting Indian dress, vegetarianism, celibacy, or a host of other massive changes in lifestyle. Incidentally, Western monastics did and still do the same.

This is just the sort of preaching that frightens so many people. They get the idea that practicing meditation leads inexorably to a withdrawal from society, into some strange and exotic sect. Meditation becomes the "fatal glass of beer," the one drink that leads to alcoholism and ruination, or the one marijuana cigarette that leads to heroin addiction and a life of crime.

There is an irony in the attempt of some enthusiastic meditators to cast aside large portions of Western civilization. While they try to adopt what they believe to be Oriental lifestyles, the countries in which these lifestyles originated are vigorously trying to import Western technology. Japan, the home of Zen, is the most aggressively technological of all Oriental nations. Indeed its level of technology has surpassed that of many Western nations. India, mired in centuries of poverty and despair, is painfully trying to raise its standard of living, largely through the use of Western methods.

Meditative practices are centuries old. And for centuries the vast majority of mankind has accepted poverty, hunger, disease, pain, and early death as their lot in this world. The passive

Meditation has often helped people accept lives filled with pain and suffering.

attitude typical of meditation may have helped to bring about this acceptance. We no longer have to accept such a prospect.

Those who wish to throw aside the Western way of life with its anxieties and stress-related diseases should remind themselves that plague and famine were regular features of simpler and more spiritual societies. So were god-kings.

While there may be great value in a technique like meditation, even in the modern world, we certainly do not have to accept all of the trappings from other ages and other cultures. Must we turn ourselves into poor replicas of twelfth-century Indian holy men, or fifteenth-century Japanese monks, to meditate properly? The problem is to try and separate what is important and useful in the practice from what is nonessential and potentially even harmful.

The Sufis, as usual, have a story which illustrates this point.

MEDITATION: WHAT IT CAN DO FOR YOU

A wise man, the wonder of his age, taught his disciples from a seemingly inexhaustible store of wisdom.

He attributed all his knowledge to a thick tome which was kept in a place of honour in his room.

The sage would allow nobody to open the volume.

When he died, those who had surrounded him, regarding themselves as his heirs, ran to open the book, anxious to possess what it contained.

They were surprised, confused and disappointed when they found that there was writing on only one page.

They became even more bewildered, and then annoyed when they tried to penetrate the meaning of the phrase which met their eyes.

It was: "When you realize the difference between the container and the content, you will have knowledge."

7

Meditation and Miracles

Holy men, particularly those who were ascetic and spent much time in meditation and prayer, have traditionally acquired the reputation of being miracle workers. Christianity in particular has a rich tradition of tales of saintly miracles.

A fourth-century biography of St. Paul the Hermit (died 347) tells of one day, "as St. Anthony himself would tell, there came suddenly to his mind the thought that no better monk than he had dwelling in the desert. But as he lay quiet that night it was revealed to him that there was deep in the desert another better by far than he, and that he must make haste to visit him."

So Anthony set out, not knowing where he was going. Somehow miraculously he found the hidden cave in which Paul was living. Paul greeted Anthony with the words, "From old time, my brother, I have known that thou wouldst come to me." Since Paul knew that his own death was near, he asked Anthony to bring back a special cloak that Bishop Athanasius had given to him in which to wrap his body. Anthony was astounded that

Paul could have known of the cloak at all. Once again he set off. But on his return journey he had a vision of Paul "climbing the steps of heaven," and knew that Paul had died. On reaching Paul's cave, he found the lifeless body still kneeling as if in prayer.

St. Joseph of Copertino was a seventeenth-century Italian monk known for his simple piety and fierce asceticism. He was also reported to have regularly levitated and floated about the room in full view of many witnesses. In addition, Joseph was said to possess the ability to read people's minds and foresee the future.

Not only Christian saints were credited with such powers. Paramahansa Yogananda was an Indian yogi who lived and taught in the U.S. for many years until his death in 1952. His book, *Autobiography of a Yogi,* is probably the most popular single work on the life of a yogi to appear in English. In it Yogananda recounts a tale of the first meeting of two celebrated gurus, Lahiri Mahasaya and his master Babaji. Lahiri was walking through the hills one day when he heard his name being called. He followed the voice for miles to a hidden cave where Babaji awaited him. Babaji told him that in his past life Lahiri had lived in that same cave and had been Babaji's disciple. He stayed with Babaji ten days, but after that Babaji would appear to him when his guidance was needed.

Yogananda himself reported receiving telepathic messages and visions from his own master, Sri Yukteswar, a disciple of Lahiri.

Baba Ram Dass, formerly Professor Richard Alpert of Harvard, recalled a number of occasions in which the personal guru that he had found in India appeared able to read his mind.

Tibet, until its takeover by the Chinese Communists, had been

the home of a particular, and very exotic, form of Buddhism. The monks or lamas there were routinely credited with miraculous powers. For example, in a biography of the eleventh-century lama Naropa, it is reported how Naropa was meditating when he saw a bright light. Then he had a vision that his successor to be was a certain novice monk named Marpa staying at a distant monastery. When a messenger was sent to the monastery it was discovered that a novice monk named Marpa was indeed staying there, though Naropa had no way of knowing this through ordinary means.

All of these tales can be set aside as simple folklore. There is no way to verify them. In retelling events people tend to prefer the wonderful to the ordinary, particularly where holy men are concerned. Yet it must be admitted that stories of this nature are extremely persistent.

We must also recognize that no major religion actually denies the possibility of miracles. There is, however, considerable disagreement as to how often and under what conditions miracles may take place.

Most common folk expect miracles from those of great holiness. It is the final and absolute proof of holiness. The Biblical admonition "Lest ye see miracles ye will not believe" recognizes this fact of human nature.

Yet often holy men treat miracles with a sort of lofty disdain, as though they represent a lesser form of spirituality, when compared to meditation. Two tales, one from Buddhism, the other from the Sufi, illustrate this point.

Gautama the Buddha was sitting with his disciples discussing the problems of inner development. A man interrupted the discussion and said that he could do the most marvelous thing, he

The Buddha

MEDITATION AND MIRACLES

could fly. To demonstrate, he rose from the ground and flew around the room.

The Buddha looked on impassively. When the demonstration was finished, the Buddha turned back to his discussion of more important matters.

A would-be disciple went to Bahaudin.

The master was surrounded by thirty of his students, in a garden after dinner.

The newcomer said, "I wish to serve you."

Bahaudin answered, "You can best serve me by reading my *Risalat* [Letters]."

"I have already done so," said the newcomer.

"If you had done so in reality and not in appearance you would not have approached me in this manner," said Bahaudin.

He continued, "Why do you think that you are able to learn?"

"I am ready to study with you."

Bahaudin said, "Let the most junior Murid [disciple] stand up."

Anwari, who was sixteen years of age, rose to his feet.

"How long have you been with us?" asked El-Shah.

"Three weeks, O Murshid."

"Have I taught you anything?"

"I do not know."

"Do you think so?"

"I do not think so."

Bahaudin said to him:

"In this newcomer's satchel you will find a book of poems. Take it in your hand and recite the entire contents without mistake and without even opening it."

Anwari found the book. He did not open it, but said: "I fear that it is in Turki."

A Sufi of the seventeenth or eighteenth century

Bahaudin said, "Recite it!"

Anwari did so, and as he finished the stranger became more and more affected by this wonder—a book being read without being opened by someone who did not know Turki.

Falling at the feet of Bahaudin, he begged to be admitted to the Circle.

Bahaudin said, "It is this kind of phenomenon which attracts you—while it still does, you cannot really benefit from it. That is why, even if you have read my *Risalat*, you have not really read it.

"Come back," he continued, "when you have read it as this beardless boy has read it. It was only such study that gave him

the power to recite from a book which he had not opened, and at the same time prevented him from groveling in wonderment at the event."

To perform miracles, and then to casually wave them aside as accomplishments of little merit, is of course an awesome display of power. It is very much like the rich man lighting his cigars with $100 bills. It makes the miracles ever so much more attractive. It also provides a convenient excuse for not performing them on demand. "Of course, I could perform a miracle, but I don't engage in such vulgar and immature activities."

None of the currently popular meditation systems promises that the devotee will be able to perform miracles. There are, however, a number of groups which exist on the fringes of the meditation movement, which do promise "psychic powers" to those who adopt their particular system. Moreover, meditators often privately tell one another tales of the miraculous accomplishments of this or that guru. It is all part of the guru-worship syndrome. The Bible was quite right. "Lest ye see miracles ye will not believe" is the unacknowledged motto of many.

A childlike belief that the master can perform miracles has occasionally been carried to grotesque and terrifying lengths. Recently a grisly story about a cult broke into the headlines in New York City. The group had originally formed primarily to study and practice meditation under the leadership of a strong and charismatic individual. As time went on this leader began to claim greater and greater powers. Finally he even said that he knew how to raise the dead.

When one member of the group died of cancer, other members stood around the body praying and chanting in order to return

their dead friend to life. This went on for weeks. It was only when the body actually began to rot, and the neighbors to complain, that the story came out.

The incident is bizarre, insane, and yet the members of the group were all apparently intelligent, well-educated, and quite sane.

Do spiritual exercises like meditation give certain people the power to perform miracles? First, we must decide what a miracle is. Roughly defined, a miracle is an event or an act above or beyond the generally understood laws of nature.

We have already discussed how certain yogis are able to still their hearts and lower their metabolism, accomplishments once thought to be beyond the natural operation of the human body. But such accomplishments can now be explained in terms of conventional physiology, by merely enlarging our concept of what degree of control the conscious mind possesses over the physical body.

Seeing the future, or rising up and floating around the room, are events which cannot be explained in any conventional terms, no matter how much we enlarge the concepts. Such phenomena represent an overturning of natural laws as we currently understand them. People who believe in such phenomena insist, however, that they are not supernatural at all, and they are merely labeled such because scientists are currently unable to explain them. When they can be explained, runs this argument, they are classed as natural. Raising the dead is still considered a genuine miracle by almost anyone's standards.

This gets us into the matter of language. "Miracle" is no longer a fashionable word. "Supernatural" isn't much better. Today when one wishes to discuss such things as mind reading, or seeing into the future, or even levitating, they are more likely

to be described as abilities that are psychic or paranormal or extrasensory. The words sound more scientific than "miracle." The message St. Anthony received from St. Paul was once called a miracle or a vision. Today it would be called an example of telepathy or ESP.

There is not much that can be done in the way of verifying accounts of the psychic abilities of saints who died hundreds of years ago. There isn't even much that can be done to investigate the reported abilities of some of today's gurus. But many ordinary meditators have also reported having psychic experiences during meditation, or in having their psychic abilities improved by meditation.

One study, undertaken by Karlis Osis and Edwin Bokert of the American Society for Psychical Research, appears to support some of these beliefs. Testing ESP ability directly after people had finished meditating, the one factor they found to be most strongly correlated with ESP was "self-transcendence and openness"—a key quality that marks the successful meditator.

In theory, at least, meditation should enhance psychic ability. A large percentage of the extrasensory experiences that are reported come during sleep, or in a period of quiet reverie. Rarely are such events reported to occur during the middle of a busy day. The reason for this, according to much psychic theory, is that at such quiet moments the flow of impulses through the ordinary senses is extremely low or, as some put it, the background sensory "noise" is reduced. It is then that the consciousness should be open to more subtle extrasensory impressions, or to other "energies." If this is the case for sleep and quiet reverie, it should be more so for meditation. In deep meditation the level of sensory "noise" should be turned even lower than it is in sleep, and the consciousness expanded delib-

erately to catch whispers from beyond the normal sensory realm.

It is a theory that sounds reasonable. But is it true? Is there sufficient hard evidence to back the claim that meditation enhances psychic abilities? There are many intriguing stories, to be sure. These may be highly significant. But it is rather sobering to remember that there were once many intriguing stories about the unicorn. And the unicorn does not exist, and never did.

The problem lies not primarily in deciding whether meditation helps to develop psychic abilities, but in whether such abilities exist at all. Many people who believe deeply in psychic phenomena speak rather glibly of how their existence has been "proved scientifically." True, psychic abilities have been investigated scientifically. In fact, such investigations have been going on for nearly a century. But there is considerable controversy over whether such investigations have produced conclusive proof.

Some scientists are convinced that abilities like telepathy and precognition (seeing the future) have been adequately demonstrated in the laboratory. An equal number hold that all of the experiments and studies have proved absolutely nothing, and that it is reasonable to conclude after all this time that such phenomena do not exist. The majority of scientists probably hold opinions somewhere between these two. They feel that the experiments have turned up some interesting results, but that the case is far from having been proved.

One thing that a century of research into psychic phenomena has certainly proved is that it is a very difficult area to work with under laboratory conditions. If the phenomena exist at all, they are delicate and elusive.

When we try and add meditation to this already difficult and complex problem, the experimental situation becomes even

MEDITATION AND MIRACLES

more difficult and complex, and the results more ambiguous. The Osis-Bokert study indicated that good meditators are good at ESP, yet the final word on ESP is not in yet, and there is not even any general agreement as to who is a good meditator. The field of psychical research is hopelessly muddled at the moment.

Perhaps some day we will arrive at scientifically acceptable answers for all of the questions about meditation and psychic phenomena. But that day is not yet at hand, nor have we any good reason to believe that it will come soon.

The most sensible thing that anyone can do is to suspend judgment. Don't be dazzled by miracle tales of magical gurus. Don't even pay much attention to paranormal events that seem to occur during your own meditation program. Virtually every school of meditation training warns that the novice should not be sidetracked by such experiences. Besides, the ability of the human mind to deceive itself into thinking something paranormal has occurred, when the event can be explained by other means, is practically boundless.

Learn from the story of the Buddha. Ignore the man flying around the room, and turn your attention to more important matters.

8

Meditation, Mysticism, and the Right Hemisphere

People meditate for many different reasons. In America today a lot of people have taken up the practice because it helps them to relax, reduce stress, and hopefully improve their health.

Another commonly given reason for meditation is that it makes people feel better, not physically, but emotionally and psychologically. They hope to be able to approach the tasks of daily life with a calmer and clearer mind, and with an improved ability to concentrate, and not be distracted by extraneous events.

These are perfectly reasonable goals, and there is considerable evidence that meditation can be helpful in attaining them. But such goals are also limited. They are certainly not what the saints, and dervishes, and roshis, and lamas have been after for centuries.

Others go into meditation for less credible reasons. They meditate because it has become fashionable, or because they

have fallen under the spell of a popular and powerful leader. That is foolish at best and, in some cases, destructive.

Some people have come to believe that meditation is a royal road to personal happiness or to becoming more creative. They are doomed to ultimate disappointment.

Then there are a lot of people who meditate for "kicks," because they think that they are going to get some sort of "high" or "peak experience." Such people overvalue some of the novel feelings that meditation can produce.

There are those who seek visions, or believe that they will become psychic. Yet for centuries virtually all the serious teachers of meditative practices, no matter what tradition they come from, have warned that such hopes are diversions, and even dangers to the meditator.

Now so far we have said a good deal about what the goals of meditation are not. But what *is* the goal of perfected meditation? The word one runs across most often is, Nothing. This may seem paradoxical, and rather startling, yet it can be abundantly documented.

One can even find evidence of such a goal in the writings of TM founder, Maharishi Mahesh Yogi, the most optimistic and aggressively modern of teachers of meditation. The Maharishi writes that eventually the meditator discovers that the world is "based on a never-changing element of no-form and no-phenomenon."

Satori, the state of "enlightenment" in Zen Buddhism, has also often been described as a "blank mind" state.

The fourteenth-century monk who wrote *The Cloud of Unknowing* wrote, "And so keep on working in this nothingness which is nowhere and do not try to involve your body's senses or their proper objects."

The Buddhist Nagarjuna said: "The teacher [Gautama] has taught that a 'becoming' and a 'non-becoming' are destroyed; therefore it obtains that: nirvana is neither an existent thing nor an unexistent thing."

A tale attributed to Chuang Tzu, an early Taoist philosopher, makes much the same point:

Yen Hui said, "I have made some progress."

"What do you mean?" asked Confucius.

"I have forgotten humanity and righteousness," replied Yen Hui.

"Very good, but that is not enough," said Confucius.

On another day Yen Hui saw Confucius again and said, "I have made some progress."

"What do you mean?" asked Confucius.

"I have forgotten ceremonies and music," replied Yen Hui.

"Very good, but that is not enough," said Confucius.

Another day Yen Hui saw Confucius again and said, "I have made some progress."

"What do you mean?" asked Confucius.

Yen Hui said, "I forget everything while sitting down."

Confucius' face turned pale. He said, "What do you mean by sitting down and forgetting everything?"

"I cast aside my limbs," replied Yen Hui, "discard my intelligence, detach from both body and mind, and become one with the Great Universal [Tao]. This is called sitting down and forgetting everything."

Confucius said, "When you become one with the Great Universal, you will have no partiality, and when you are part of the process of transformation, you will have no constancy. You are really a worthy man. I beg to follow your steps."

... AND THE RIGHT HEMISPHERE

This brief list of negatives could be extended almost endlessly with examples drawn from almost every age, religion, philosophy, and language.

Another concept often encountered in the writings of advanced meditators is "killing the ego" or "annihilation of the self." The idea seems to be destroying all sense of individuality. In the West, which has been strongly individualistic for several hundred years, such concepts seem alien, and antihuman.

But is this negative, mindless antihumanism really what the deeply committed meditator seeks? No, it is not. It only sounds that way because we are again trapped in a language problem. You may recall that in the very first chapter I warned that the inner experience of perfected meditation was not the sort of thing that one could talk about. All meditative traditions insist on this one fact at least. Yet many have talked about this experience at great length. What they have said so often sounds very negative and depressing. Why?

California psychiatrist Claudio Narnjo has been a student of ancient and modern systems of meditation. In assessing the overwhelmingly negative impression that seems to be attached to the perfected states of meditation he observed:

"Since the goal of meditation is precisely something beyond the bounds of our customary experience, anything that we might understand would probably be something that is not, and an attachment to the understanding could only prevent progress. This is why many traditions have discouraged descriptions, avoided images or positive formulations of man's perfected state or of the deity, and stressed either practice or negative formulations."

Regular meditation is still part of the lives of monks of rigorous religious orders like the Cistercians of the Strict Observance in Melbourne, Australia. Other forms of meditation are new to the West. Vilayat Khan leads a Sufi community in New Lebanon, New York, on the site of an early Shaker settlement (opposite).

In other words, we can't describe it. To try would only confuse matters and mislead us. If we feel we must try, the best we can do is say what it isn't. That is why writings on the subject often seem so paradoxical and negative. The writer is trying to describe the indescribable. The harder he tries the more confusing and unlike the experience the description becomes, so he says that it is like nothing.

A fifth-century Christian mystic called Dionysius the Areopagite stated the problem this way:

"It is named Invisible, Infinite, and Unbounded, in such

terms as may indicate not what It is, but what It is not: for this, in my judgment, is more in accord with its nature, since, as the capital mysteries and the priestly traditions suggested, we are right in saying that It is not in the likeness of any created thing, and we cannot comprehend Its superessential, invisible, and ineffable infinity. If, therefore, the negations in the descriptions of the divine are true, and the affirmations are inconsistent with It. . ."

Evelyn Underhill, a twentieth-century Englishwoman who was both a mystic and an influential writer on the subject of mysticism, decisively rejected the idea that perfected states of meditation were negative in any sense, at least in Christian tradition.

"The doctrine of annihilation as the end of the soul's ascent, whatever the truth may be as to the Moslem attitude concerning it, is decisively rejected by all European mystics, though a belief in it is constantly being imputed to them by their enemies: for their aim is not suppression of life, but its intensification, a change in its form. This change, they say in a paradox which is generally misunderstood, consists in the perfection of the personality by the utter surrender of self. It is true that the more Orientally-minded amongst them. . .do use language of a negative kind which seems almost to involve a belief in annihilation rather than the transformation of the self in God: but this is because they are trying to describe a condition of supersensible vitality from the point of view of the normal consciousness, to which it can only seem a Nothing, a Dark, a Self-loss."

Two other concepts also frequently associated with higher or perfected states of meditation are "enlightenment" or "illumination," and "mysticism." Enlightenment or illumination means that the person has learned something, presumably something of great value. Mysticism is one way in which some-

thing is learned. It is knowledge received directly, without going through the usual step by step mental processes. The whole process is explained with a clarity unusual in mystic writing by Al-Ghazali, an eleventh-century Sufi.

"Let the worshipper reduce his heart to a state in which the existence of anything and its nonexistence are the same to him. Then let him sit alone in some corner, limiting his religious duties to what is absolutely necessary, and not occupying himself either with reciting the Koran or considering its meaning or with books of religious traditions or with anything of the sort. And let him see to it that nothing save God most High enters his mind. Then, as he sits in solitude, let him not cease saying continuously with his tongue, 'Allah, Allah,' keeping his thought on it. At last he will reach a state when the motion of his tongue will cease, and it will seem as though the word flowed from it. Let him persevere in this until all trace of motion is removed from his tongue, and he finds his heart persevering in the thought. Let him still persevere until the form of the word, its letters and shape, is removed from his heart, and there remains the idea alone, as though clinging to his heart, inseparable from it. So far, all is dependent on his will and choice; but to bring the mercy of God does not stand in his will or choice. He has now laid himself bare to the breathings of that mercy, and nothing remains but to wait what God will open to him, as God has done after this manner to prophets and saints. If he follows the above course, he may be sure that the light of the Real will shine out in his heart."

Mysticism is a practice which has fallen into disrepute, at least in the West. To many people it has come to mean knowledge that is obscure, often deliberately so, or downright fraudulent. The mystic is supposed to receive his information in a sudden

flash of inspiration, or as a "revelation." But inspirations and revelations are highly suspect today. They have come to be regarded as primitive, emotional, or the result of just plain sloppy thinking. The mystic way of arriving at conclusions is now considered distinctly inferior to information or conclusions arrived at through reasoning and logic.

Indeed mysticism itself is looked upon with considerable distrust because many believe it leads to fanaticism, even madness. It brings knowledge to which the tests of reason and logic cannot be applied. You cannot argue with a mystic.

Yet there is a strong thread of mysticism that runs throughout all of human history. In some periods it is taken more seriously than in others. The highest state of meditation is surely a mystical one. In suppressing all of the ordinary modes of sense and thought the individual is opened to the mystic experience, what Al-Ghazali called "the light of the Real."

One of the great mysteries of mysticism was that no one could figure out what happened during a mystical state. Mystics couldn't describe it and science couldn't measure it. So people began to assume that nothing happened, at least nothing worthwhile. But, ironically, modern science, which has so long denigrated mysticism as unimportant, may now be providing some insights into how it works.

In an earlier chapter I mentioned the fact that the human brain possesses two halves or hemispheres, and that this fact may prove to be very significant in the study of meditation. Here is why.

The two-hemisphere structure of the human brain is immediately obvious to anyone who sees a photograph or looks at a model of the brain. The two halves are connected by a thick bundle of nerve fibers, and they look identical. But for well over

... AND THE RIGHT HEMISPHERE

a century scientists have realized that the functions of the brain's two hemispheres are not identical.

The brain's control over the body is "crossed," that is, the left hemisphere controls the muscular action and visual and auditory space on the right half of the body; the right hemisphere exercises control over the left. But that is not all.

People who had received severe injuries to the left half of their brain often lost the ability to speak. Injuries to the right half of the brain almost never produced speech loss. Language ability was centered in the left hemisphere of the brain. Gradually it became apparent that the left hemisphere of the brain controlled not only language, but also mathematics, and logic. But what were the special functions of the right hemisphere?

For a while it seemed as though the right hemisphere didn't have any special functions. But as the problem was looked at more closely the particular talents controlled by the brain's right hemisphere began to reveal themselves. For example, a person who had an injury to the right half of his brain might be able to talk perfectly well, but was unable to dress himself properly. People who had right brain injuries had difficulties with facial recognition tests. The right brain controlled spatial abilities. But since the right brain did not control the language, it couldn't "talk," and couldn't communicate its functions on tests which depend primarily on language. That is why it took psychologists so long to figure out what it was good for.

Psychologists have now developed some fairly simple tests which indicate which half of the brain dominates during different mental tasks. Here is one you can try on your friends. Ask a friend to spell Mississippi. He usually will make more eye movements to the right (controlled by the left half of the brain). If you ask him to imagine what the river looks like, however, he

will make more eye movements to the left. The shape of a river is a spatial problem.

There is now a fairly substantial body of evidence to indicate that the two hemispheres of the brain control two distinctly different ways of thinking. The left half emphasizes words and logic. It takes information in bits, step by step, and builds a conclusion. This is what psychologists call "linear thinking." The right half does not appear to engage in step-by-step thinking; it takes in the entire picture all at once. Right brain thinking is more intuitive. If you think of the Mississippi River you do not build the picture bit by bit, the whole picture comes into your head.

Both types of thought are needed for proper function of the brain, and each hemisphere of the brain contains some of the abilities controlled by the other. The distinction between the functions of the two halves of the brain is not as simple as it can be made to sound.

But still, in most of us one hemisphere or the other tends to dominate the way we think. Lawyers and scientists appear to use their left brain more than their right, whereas artists and musicians are more right-brained. So are successful athletes and dancers. They do not analyze the moves they make.

It is only fair to remark, at this point, that much of the information about right- and left-thinking is quite new, and the theories about different modes of thought are speculative. Not everyone is persuaded by the evidence presented to date. But the theories have attracted a good deal of scientific attention and support. And they do seem to explain some of the puzzles of human consciousness.

While many higher animals have right and left hemispheres

to their brains, human beings seem to be the only animals in which the two hemispheres control two different types of thought. Moreover, the dominance of one hemisphere of the brain over the other is not inborn. It is something that we develop as we grow up.

In young children the two halves of the brain serve functions that are more nearly identical. If a child under the age of about six receives an injury to the left half of his brain and loses his speech, he can generally regain it with time. The right half of the brain takes over for the injured left. In an adult the centers of control are too firmly fixed. The right hemisphere can no longer take over, and recovery from an injury is impossible.

Let's carry the theory a step further. If individuals can learn to be predominately left-brained or right-brained, so can societies. The West, since the time of the Renaissance has been a heavily left-brained society. We prefer the logical and verbal methods of approaching problems, as opposed to the intuitive. While we may also respect artists and musicians, we do not necessarily think of them as being intelligent, merely creative. One psychologist said that we are so much in awe of verbal intelligence that when we say that someone has a great mind, we all too often mean only that he has a great mouth.

Robert Ornstein is the nation's leading exponent of the theory of right- and left-brain thinking. He has said:

"The complementary workings of our two thought processes permit our highest achievements, but most occupations value one mode over the other. Science and law, for example, emphasize linear thought and verbal logic. The arts, religions, and music are more present-oriented, aconceptual, and intuitive. The

unfortunate result is that many intellectuals often disparage the nonverbal mind, while many mystics and poets often disparage the rational mind."

All of those activities which we have classified as meditation, be they sittting quietly repeating a mantra, or whirling and chanting, may have a common physiological basis and a common purpose. They are centered primarily in the right hemisphere of the brain and they may be used to train people in the use of the right hemisphere, to give new and important perspectives on human existence and the relationship of the individual to his own body and to the universe.

One can build an intriguing case for mysticism as a right-brained activity. The mystic experience is nonverbal, and nonlogical; so is the right brain. The mystic experiences a union with God, or the Universe or the Tao, or whatever one wishes to call It. The left brain builds step by step, while the right brain takes in the whole picture. The mystic knows he is experiencing Reality, but cannot explain it. The right brain is intuitive. And so on. Such comparisons do not constitute proof positive by any means, but they are suggestive.

For the first time in history we may have some basis for understanding how and why ancient practices like meditation really work. You might say that the left brain has begun to analyze the workings of the right brain. But to discover that the mental aspects of a practice like meditation take place primarily in the right brain should not reduce their importance. On the contrary, it should make us wonder if one-half of our brain is not seriously underemployed most of the time.

Meditators often speak of the practice as a means of "opening the third eye," or "energizing the chakras." It may be more

... AND THE RIGHT HEMISPHERE

accurate to say that meditation is a process which trains us in the use of the right hemisphere of our brain.

Just knowing where the activity takes place does not really explain it, nor does it teach us how to use the right hemisphere. Knowing that language is primarily a left-brained activity is useful, but that does not constitute learning a language. We still must study grammar, spelling, writing, etc. So it may be with right-brained activities. We still must study the techniques, like meditation, which activate the right brain.

Many of those who seriously practice meditation speak of it as a means of increasing their "self-knowledge" or of "becoming whole." If we consider meditation training in the proper use of half of the human brain, then such statements may not be mere metaphors or vague hopes.

Our modern Western world is dominated by the scientists and the lawyers, not by the mystics and poets. The result has been, in the view of men like Robert Ornstein, a society dominated to an unhealthy degree by a left-brained mode of thinking, one which downplays or ignores half of human consciousness. "We must not ignore the right hemisphere talents," he has written, "which in the long run may prove essential to our personal and cultural survival."

9

Life Is a Fountain

There was a young man who was profoundly dissatisfied with his existence. If one just looked at his life from the outside it seemed as though he had everything—an excellent job, a beautiful apartment, plenty of money, interesting friends, and all the other things that, according to the values of modern society, should make him happy. But he wasn't happy. He didn't know what life really was.

The young man decided that the wisest person he had ever met was his old professor at Harvard. So one day he walked off his job and went to Harvard to visit his old professor.

"Professor," the young man said, "what is life?"

"My boy," the professor answered, "I have pondered that question for many years and am no closer to the answer now than I ever was. The wisest man that I ever met was my old tutor at Oxford. Maybe he can help you."

So the young man hopped on a plane bound for England and located the tutor in his book-lined study.

"What is life?" he asked.

LIFE IS A FOUNTAIN

The tutor puffed on his pipe for a moment, then said, "In all my years of study I have not been able to come close to an answer for that question. But I spent some time in India, and there I met an extremely wise holy man. If anyone in the world can help you it should be that man."

So the young man went to India and, after great difficulties and considerable expense, he located the wise man sitting by the roadside in a small village.

"Great teacher, what is life?" asked the young man.

The old, bearded man shook his head sadly. "I have spent my life in meditation, but the answer to that question has eluded me. There is only one person in the world who may help you. He is a hermit who lives in a cave high in the mountains. I have never met him but he is said to be the wisest person on earth."

The young man, now obsessed by his quest, set off for the mountains. Crossing the desert he lost his way, and nearly died of hunger and thirst. When he came to the mountains they were even more terrible. At one point he nearly froze to death. At another he barely escaped being crushed in an avalanche. And several times he was near plunging to his death.

But finally he reached a remote cave, in which sat an incredibly ancient and emaciated sage, wrapped in a blanket.

"O Master of All Knowledge," gasped the young man, "I have given up all my worldly goods. I have traveled thousands of miles. I have endured great hardships and faced death many times, all to find the answer to one question, 'What is life?' "

The ancient sage opened his eyes slowly and said softly, "Life is a fountain."

The young man let this sink in for a moment. And then he jumped up and shouted, "I've come all this way, and all you can tell me is 'Life is a fountain'?"

The sage was amazed. "You mean life isn't a fountain?"

MEDITATION: WHAT IT CAN DO FOR YOU

That is not a Sufi teaching tale. Nor is it a parable drawn from the accumulated folk wisdom of any other people. It's just an old American joke, and perhaps not a very funny one at that. But like teaching tales and parables, this old joke makes a point.

Meditation has come or, to be more accurate, come back, to the West. It has arrived preceded by a long list of promises about the great things that it can do, and hidden in an exotic, but tantalizing cloud of mystery.

In fact, it is beginning to look as if meditation can do a great deal. Its usefulness in promoting relaxation is fairly well documented.

Its ability to produce novel, and perhaps enlightening, mental experiences for the meditator is beyond question.

Most important, it may very well be one key to unlocking a vast area of human consciousness. This can't be said with any certainty yet, but the prospects are encouraging.

But it doesn't provide THE ANSWER. Not for most of us, not today. Our society is too complicated, and the human race now has too much knowledge and control of the external world to be satisfied solely with internal solutions.

We cannot abandon the accomplishments of rationalism and science or, if you like, of the left hemisphere of the human brain. These accomplishments have been magnificent.

Nor can we assume that all of our current problems have grown out of the rationalistic approach to life. Plenty of mystics have preached holy war in the past. But it is no longer wise to try and ignore the nonrational side of the brain as unimportant either. We have to try and find some sort of balance, and that's not going to be easy.

We Americans are, alas, addicted to the quick fix, the "in-

stant, no sweat, no hassle solution to all your problems." A century ago medicine show promoters made a fortune peddling an astonishing variety of old (American) Indian cure-alls, and secret nostrums that were supposed to be good for whatever ailed you. The remedies didn't work, but people kept right on buying them anyway, because they promised so much and were so easy to take.

Ancient wisdom, once scorned and reviled in the West, is now making a comeback. And on the whole that's a good thing. We have even forgotten that there is considerable merit in just sitting quietly for a while.

But since we lack experience with techniques like meditation we are in danger of misunderstanding what is presented to us. We are a little like the natives of some remote island when first shown the fruits of Western technology. It is difficult for us to tell the difference between a string of glass beads and something of real use and value. There is a genuine danger of our being misled and exploited.

The backbiting and badmouthing of competing gurus and learned masters should be enough to put us on our guard. Each claims to be in possession of the genuine article, and says that his rival's wares are shoddy fakes.

Should you take up meditation?

That, of course, is a question that only you can answer. Over the last few years millions of Americans have answered a resounding yes to the question.

Some have been disappointed and disillusioned by meditation. But many, many more feel that they have received great benefit from their rediscovery of this ancient practice.

Bibliography

Benson, Herbert and Klipper, Miriam Z. *The Relaxation Response.* New York: Morrow, 1975.

Bloomfield, Harold H., Cain, M. P., Jaffe, D. T., and Kory, R. B. *TM—Discovering Inner Energy and Overcoming Stress.* New York: Dell, 1975.

Bloomfield, Harold H. and Kory, R. B. *Happiness—the TM Program for Psychiatry and Enlightenment.* New York: Simon and Schuster, 1976.

Cameron, Charles (ed.). *Who Is Guru Maharaj Ji?* New York: Bantam, 1973.

Campbell, Anthony. *TM and the Nature of Enlightenment.* New York: Perennial Library, 1976.

Campbell, Colin. "Transcendence Is As American As Ralph Waldo Emerson." *Psychology Today.* April, 1974.

Cohen, Daniel. *Dreams, Visions and Drugs.* New York: Watts, 1976.

———. *The Far Side of Consciousness.* New York: Dodd, Mead, 1975.

———. *The New Believers.* New York: Evans, 1976.

Denniston, Denise and McWilliams, Peter. *The TM Book.* Los Angeles: Price/Stern/Sloan, 1975.

BIBLIOGRAPHY

Ebon, Martin. "Arica Goes Public." *Transcendental Meditation Today*. September, 1976.

———. *Maharishi, The Founder of Transcendental Meditation*. New York: NAL, 1975.

———. *The Relaxation Controversy*. New York: NAL, 1976.

Evans, Christopher. *Cults of Unreason*. New York: Farrar, Straus and Giroux, 1973.

Goleman, Daniel. "Meditation Helps Break the Stress Spiral." *Psychology Today*. February, 1976.

Hemingway, Patricia Drake. *The Transcendental Meditation Primer*. New York: McKay, 1975.

James, William. *The Varieties of Religious Experience*. New York: Crowell-Collier, 1958.

Jonas, Gerald. *Visceral Learning*. New York: Viking, 1973.

Kamiya, Joseph. "Conscious Control of Brain Waves." *Psychology Today*. April, 1968.

Kapleau, Philip (ed.). *The Three Pillars of Zen*. Boston: Beacon, 1965.

Karlins, Marvin and Andrews, Lewis M. *Biofeedback: Turning on the Power of Your Mind*. Philadelphia: Lippincott, 1972.

Lawrence, Jodi. *Alpha Brain Waves*. Los Angeles: Nash, 1972.

LeShan, Lawrence. *How to Meditate*. Boston: Little, Brown, 1974.

Lilly, John C. *The Center of the Cyclone*. New York: Bantam, 1973.

Luce, G. G. and Peper, E. "Mind over Body, Body over Mind." *The New York Times Magazine*. September 12, 1971.

Maharishi Mahesh Yogi. *Transcendental Meditation*. New York: NAL, 1968.

Naranjo, Claudio and Ornstein, Robert. *The Psychology of Meditation*. New York: Viking, 1971.

Needleman, Jacob. *The New Religions*. New York: Doubleday, 1970.

Ornstein, Robert. *The Mind Field*. New York: Grossman/Viking, 1976.

BIBLIOGRAPHY

———(ed.). *The Nature of Human Consciousness.* New York: Viking, 1974.

———. *The Psychology of Consciousness.* San Francisco: W. H. Freeman, 1972.

———. "Right and Left Thinking." *Psychology Today.* May, 1973.

Otis, Leon. "If Well Integrated but Anxious, Try TM." *Psychology Today.* April, 1974.

Scarf, Maggie. "Tuning Down with TM." *The New York Times Magazine.* February, 9, 1975.

Schwartz, Gary. "TM Relaxes Some People and Makes Them Feel Better." *Psychology Today.* April, 1974.

Shah, Idries. *The Way of the Sufi.* New York: Dutton, 1969.

———. *Thinkers of the East.* Baltimore: Penguin, 1972.

———.*Wisdom of the Idiots.* New York: Dutton, 1971.

Shainberg, Lawrence. "The Violence of 'Just Sitting'." *The New York Times Magazine.* October 10, 1976.

Smith, Adam. *Powers of the Mind.* New York: Random House, 1975.

Tart, Charles (ed.). *Altered States of Consciousness.* New York: Doubleday, 1972.

Underhill, Evelyn. *Mysticism.* New York: Dutton, 1961.

Wallace, R. K. "Physiological Effects of Transcendental Meditation." *Science.* March 27, 1970.

———and Benson, H. "The Physiology of Meditation." *Scientific American.* February, 1972.

White, John (ed.). *The Highest State of Consciousness.* New York: Doubleday/Anchor, 1972.

———. *What Is Meditation?* New York: Doubleday/Anchor, 1974.

Yogananda, Paramahansa. *Autobiography of a Yogi.* Los Angeles: Self-Realization Fellowship.

Index

Abulafia, Rabbi, 29
Aikido, 27
Al-Ghazali, 123, 124
Allahabad University (India), 40
All-India Institute of Medical Science, 80
Alpert, Richard (Baba Ram Dass), 88, 106
Alpha waves
  biofeedback and, 75–79
  nature of, 74–75
  yogis and, 80–81
  Zen meditators and, 81–82
American Association for the Advancement of Science, 45
American Society for Psychical Research, 113
Anis, 31
Arica, 34–35
Athanasius, Bishop, 103
Autobiography of a Yogi (Yogananda), 106

Babaji, 106
Bagchi, Basu K., 79
Bahaudin, Sufi, 109–11
Bapack (Mohammed Subuh), 36

Battelle, Phyllis, 69–70
Beach Boys (rock group), 42
"Beat Generation," 19
Beatles (rock group), 41–42
Benson, Herbert, 36, 101
  and Benson-Wallace study of effects of meditation, 44–45
  and relaxation response (RR), 59–64
Benson-Wallace meditation study, 44–45, 70
Beta waves, 74, 80
Beth Israel Hospital (Boston), 61
Bhagwan Shree Rajneesh, 52
Bible, the, 111
Biofeedback, 75–79
Bloomfield, Harold, 57, 63
Bokert, Edwin, 113
Boredom, relaxation response and, 66
Brahmanand Saraswati, Swami (Guru Dev), 41–42, 49
Brain, the
  alpha waves and, 74–82
  concentration and functioning of, 83–84
  right hemisphere of, 124–29

139

INDEX

Brainwashing, 91–94
Buddhism
  Japanese Zen, 6, 18
  in Tibet, 106–7

Cabala, the, 29
Chakras, energizing the, 17, 18, 128
Chanting, 49
  Hare Krishna use of, 12, 14, 85
Chaudhari, Haridas, 96–97
Chinese Communists, 106
Christianity
  meditation and, 3, 23–29, 87
  miracles and, 105–6
Chuang Tzu, 118
Cloud of Unknowing, The (anonymous), 24, 62, 94, 117
Concentration, brain functioning and, 83–84
Confucius, 118
Creativity, 71

Dancing
  Gurdjieff's teachings and, 33
  Sufism and, 29–30
Davis, Franklin M., 46
Delta waves, 74, 80
  deep meditation and, 77
Dev, Guru (Swami Brahmanand Saraswati), 41–42, 49
Dionysius the Areopagite, 120–22
Divine Light Mission
  criticisms of, 93–94
  practice of, 15–18
Dogen (Zen roshi), 22
Dovening, 29

Ebon, Martin, 68
Electricity, 74
Electroencephalograph (EEG), 74
  biofeedback and, 75
  measurement value of, 77–78
Enlightenment
  concentration and, 84
  defined, 122
ESP, 113–15
Evans, Christopher, 85

Farrow, Mia, 42
Fight or flight response, 60

Gallup survey (1976), 1, 38
Gautama the Buddha, 107–9, 118
Goodman, George (Adam Smith), 34–35, 50
Great Universal, the, 118
Gurdjieff, George Ivanovitch, 31–33
Guru Dev. *See* Dev, Guru

Hare Krishna (International Society for Krishna Consciousness, ISKCON)
  ban on stimulants by, 87
  chant, 12
  Evans on mantra chanting of, 85
  orthodoxy of, 91, 95
  practice of, 11–15
Hasidic Jews, 5, 29
Hatha Yoga, 11
Hesychasm, 24
High Knowledge, the, 31
Hindu Order of Shankar Acharya, 41
Hinduism
  meditation practices derived from, 9–10
  Transcendental Meditation and, 40–41, 90
Hirai, Tomio, 81
Houston Astrodome, 15
How Man Should Pray, Meister Peter, the Barber (Luther), 24

INDEX

Huxley, Aldous, 10
Hypertension, 60

Ichazo, Oskar, 34–35, 94
India
    Hinduism in, 9
    low standard of living in, 102
    Maharishi in, 40–41
    and present meditation in U.S., 1, 3
Individuality, 119
Inquisition, the, 93
International Society for Krishna Consciousness (ISKCON). *See* Hare Krishna
Islam, 23, 29–31

Japan
    Buddhism in, 3, 18
    Western technology in, 102
Jarvis, Jerry, 65, 66
Judaism, 3, 23, 29, 87

Kamiya, Joe, 75, 77, 83, 100
Kasamatsu, Akira, 81
Kelly, Ken, 93–94
Knowledge, for followers of Maharaj Ji, 16–17, 22
    criticism of, 93–94
Koan (Zen question), 21
Korean War, 91–92
Krishna, 12
Krishnamurti, 53

Ladies' Home Journal, The, 69
Lahiri Mahasaya, 106
Latihan, 36
Leary, Timothy, 88
Leisure time, 101
LeShan, Lawrence, 18, 96

Light of the Intellect, The (Abulafia), 29
Lilly, John, 34
Little Way, The (St. Theresa of Lisieux), 27
Lonborg, Jim, 47
Lotus position, 20–21
LSD, 87
Luther, Martin, 24–25

McWilliam, Peter, 65
Maharaj Ji, Guru, 15–16
    criticism of, 93–94
    on suppressing rationality, 95
Maharishi Mahesh Yogi, 11, 12, 84, 88, 94
    criticism of, 52–53
    on mantra, 56
    organization of TM by, 40–42
    on purpose of meditation, 117
    on social aims of TM, 48
Makyo experience, 84
Mantra, 1
    and Christian prayer, 23–25
    Evans on repetition of, 85
    Hare Krishna daily repetition of, 14
    and Hindu meditation, 11
    Krishnamurti's criticism of use of, 53
    relaxation response (RR) and, 61, 66–67
    TM and, 11, 49–50, 56
Marpa, 107
Meditation
    activity and, 100–1
    alpha waves and, 75–76, 78, 80–82
    antirationalism of, 95–97
    brainwashing and, 91–94
    chakras and, 17, 18, 128

INDEX

and Christianity, Judaism, and Islam, 3, 23–31
Creativity and, 71
drug use and, 87–88
ESP and, 113–15
and guru worship and submissiveness, 97, 98–100
Maharaj Ji and, 16, 17
miracles and, 111–12
negative impressions of perfected state of, 119–23
purpose of, 4–5, 90, 116–17
right hemisphere of brain and, 128–29
relaxation response (RR) and, 61–63, 66–72
Schwartz on "evolutionary precedent" for, 8
sensory deprivation and, 97–98
scientific verification of, 44–45, 70–72, 79
third eye and, 17–18, 128
TM and, 11, 51–53
varied techniques of, 1–3
Zen practice of, 20–23, 84
See also specific listings
Mind Field, The (Ornstein), 70
Miracles, 105–11, 115
Moore, C. Eugene, 68–69
Mysticism, 4
defined, 122–23
Gurdjieff and, 31–34
revelation and, 124
right hemisphere of brain and, 128–29

Nagarjuna, 118
Namath, Joe, 47
Narnjo, Claudio, 119
Naropa, 107
National Lampoon, 64

Neem Karoli Baba, Maharishi, 88
New York Times, The, 93
New York Times Magazine, The, 46

Ornstein, Robert E.
on concentration, 83–84
on guru worship, 97
on limits to use of EEG, 77
on right- and left-hemisphere thinking, 127–28, 129
on TM's "hucksterism," 70–71
Osis, Karlis, 113
Osis-Bokert study, 113, 115
Otis, Leon S., 51

Passive attitude, 101–3
Peak experience, 84
Picadilly Hotel (London), 41
Pineal body, 18
Powers of the Mind (Smith), 50
POWs (prisoners of war), 91–92
Prabhupada, 12–14, 52–53, 94
Precognition, 114
Protestants, 27
Psychedelic drugs, 87–88
Psychology Today, 8
Publishers Weekly, 64, 65
Puja (chant), 49

Quaker meeting, 27–28

Ram Dass, Baba (Richard Alpert), 88, 106
Rationalism
and antirationalism of meditation, 95–97
meditation's relation to, 99–100
Relaxation, 45
alpha state and, 75
response (RR) and TM, 59, 61–72

INDEX

Relaxation Controversy, The (Ebon), 68
Relaxation Response, The (Benson), 63–65
Religion
  drug use and, 87
  meditation's relation to, 9
  TM and, 54–56
Revelation, 124
Risalat, 109–11
Russian Revolution, 33

St. Anthony, 105–6, 113
St. Gregory of Sinai, 84–85
St. Joan, 93
St. John of the Cross, 26–27
St. Joseph of Copertino, 106
St. Paul the Hermit, 105–6, 113
Saint Theresa of Lisieux, 27
Sannyas International Movement, 52
Sanskrit, 9, 10, 49
Satori, 22–23, 117
Satsang, 16
Scarf, Maggie, 46–47, 52, 54
Scholem, Gershom, 29
Schwartz, Gary, 8, 71
Science, 44
Scientific validation
  for TM, 44–45, 70–72
  for TM and alpha biofeedback, 79
  of yogi meditation, 79–82
Sequoia National Park (California), 41
Sesshin, 20
Shah, Idries, 30–31, 109
Shainberg, Lawrence, 22
Shakers, 28
Smith, Adam (George Goodman), 34–35, 50
Stanford Research Institute, 51

Stargell, Willie, 47
Startle reaction, 80–82
Stress, 4
  TM and reduction of, 45–46, 59–60
Subud, 36
Subuh, Mohammed (Bapack), 36
Sufism, 29–31, 103–4, 109–11
Suringama Sutra, 84

Telepathy, 114
Tennyson, Alfred Lord, 34
Tension, 4, 45
Theta waves, 74
  deep meditation and, 77, 81
Thinkers of the East (Shah), 31
Third eye, opening of, 17–18, 128
Thoreau, Henry David, 87
Time, 49–50
TM, Discovering Inner Energy and Overcoming Stress, 99
Transcendental Meditation (TM), 12
  alpha biofeedback and, 78–79
  brainwashing charge and, 93
  concentration and, 83–84
  criticism of, 52–54, 88–91
  dropouts from, 51
  drug addiction and, 87
  effectiveness of, 99–100
  extensive use of, 46–47
  Hinduism and, 40–41, 90
  Maharishi's influence on, 40–42
  practice of, 11, 38–40, 47–51
  reduction of stress and, 45–46, 59–60
  relaxation response (RR) and, 60–72
  religion and, 54–56
  scientific validation and, 44–45, 70–72, 79

INDEX

Ultimate Reality, 17, 87
Underhill, Evelyn, 122
United States
  meditation in, 1
  19th century meditation in, 87
  TM practiced in, 38
  yoga practiced in, 46

Vedanta society, 10
Vedas, the, 9
  TM and, 40
Vietnam War, 92
Vivenkananda, Swami, 10

Wagner, Marion A., 79
Wallace, Robert Keith, 44, 59
"Waltons, The" (TV series), cast of, 47
Whirling dervishes, 29–30

Wordsworth, William, 36
Work ethic, 101

Yen Hui, 118
YHWH (God), 29
Yoga
  as defined in Sanskrit, 11
  as practiced in U.S., 46
Yogananda, Paramahansa, 106
Yogi, defined, 11
Yogis, scientific study of, 79–82
Yukteswar, Sri, 106

Zazen meditation
  practice of, 20–23
  scientific study of alpha waves and, 81–82
Zen, 6
  Makya experience and, 84
  as practiced in U.S., 18–23

FEB 10 1981   S

BF637   F89318   5.95
.M4C63   Cohen, Daniel.
          Meditation.

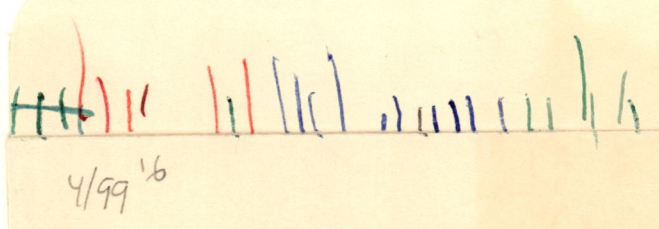

4/99 '6

Please Do Not Remove Card From Pocket
YOUR LIBRARY CARD
may be used at all library agencies. You are, of course, responsible for all materials checked out on it. As a courtesy to others please return materials promptly. A service charge is assessed for overdue materials.

The SAINT PAUL PUBLIC LIBRARY